SOLO

GETTING IT ALL TOGETHER
WHEN YOU FIND YOURSELF ALONE

ROSLYN ROMNEY REYNOLDS

BookWise
publishing

SOLO

GETTING IT ALL TOGETHER WHEN YOU FIND YOURSELF ALONE

Copyright © 2010 by Roslyn Romney Reynolds

All rights reserved.

BookWise Publishing

3138 Matterhorn Drive

West Jordan, Utah 84084

www.bookwise.com

First Edition

Book design by Eden Graphics

ISBN 978-1-60645-012-3

Library of Congress LCN 2010903919

10 9 8 7 6 5 4 3 2

Printed in the United States of America

FOR

Brooke, Erin, Anna, Hillary, Lucas, Christopher, and Megan

who all know I am never really alone.

Foreword

One moment life is normal, and one's greatest concerns are the laundry and dinner. The next moment, the phone rings and nothing is ever the same.

So it was for Roslyn Reynolds one cold January day—the day her husband drowned while on an outing with three of their children. *Solo, Getting It All Together When You Find Yourself Alone* is her story, beginning with the fateful phone call and leading to the present where she is moving forward in life with a faith in God that has given her remarkable resiliency.

The first days and weeks were dark and full of confusion, and Roslyn felt she had fallen into what C.S. Lewis described as "the dark chasm of grief."

I've known Roslyn since shortly after her husband drowned, and I have watched as she walked through and emerged from that chasm. She now shares her journey so that others taking their first timid steps into the gulf will have a little light shed on their pathway, and will know that there is, on the other end, a shaft of daylight and a new life.

Read on and find for yourself that by incorporating what she learned, there is truly hope and healing after loss.

—Richard Paul Evans, #1 *New York Times* bestselling author of *The Christmas Box* and *The Walk*

PART ONE

THE END

CHAPTER ONE

The Phone Call

"God hath not promised skies always blue . . ."

– ANNIE JOHNSON FLINT –

I was awakened from a deep sleep by the ringing of my cell phone.

"Mom, there's a problem . . ."

As my mind cleared, I realized it was Lucas' voice—our sixteen year-old son. He seemed shaken.

"What's the matter?"

"They're doing CPR on Dad."

I sat bolt upright from my nap. My breath caught, and my mind began to race. My eyes flew to the clock on the dresser—11:12 a.m. My hand clutched the phone tightly as I threw off the covers and climbed out of bed.

"Lucas, where are you? What happened?"

"We're at the Hot Springs in Honeyville, and they're not sure what happened. Can you come—now?"

I was already trying to gather things to take with me—a change of clothes in case I might need to stay in a hospital overnight with Marty, my makeup bag—but suddenly my things seemed so trivial. I slipped on some shoes, grabbed my warmest coat, my purse and the car keys, and hurried to the garage. I braced myself against the cold air as I fumbled to open the car door while trying to keep the cell phone to my ear.

"I'm on my way. Is Dad okay? Can you tell? Where are Chris and Megan? How are they?" I wanted to be sure Christopher, thirteen, and Megan, eleven, would be kept close to Lucas until I could get there.

"They're here with me. Mom, the ambulance just got here, and they're putting Dad in. They want to talk to me. Can I call you back?"

"Of course. Call as soon as you can. I'm heading there right now."

As I backed down the driveway, fear gripped my heart, and I pled with God for strength. I felt so unprepared for this. My mind was reeling, my hands shook, and my knees wobbled as I tried to shift into drive and head down the street toward the freeway on-ramp.

Father, I'm going to need you to get me there, I thought. *I don't know if I can drive feeling this way. Please be with me. Give me strength, and bless Marty and the children.*

I don't remember when I began the habit of praying anytime, anywhere. God just seemed to be someone I could call on no matter what I was doing, whether I was taking a test as a youth, looking for something I'd lost, or simply feeling inadequate. I always felt He heard my prayers and sent needed help.

I needed Him now, and as I finished my prayer, I felt a calm come over me, just enough so I could drive, and I offered a quick prayer of thanks. My mind returned to the phone call. What could have happened to Marty?

Marty. Every thought of him as I drove hurt. He and I had been through some pretty rough years recently, and we were currently separated. There had been times during the past months when I'd lost all hope of us ever making a success of our marriage, yet I somehow felt that, if only for the sake of the children, we *could* make it work. I'd seen the lives of children shattered from divorce, and I ached to think our children might end up living that nightmare. Just the night before, as I was driving up to an overnight writers' retreat for women, high in the snow-covered Utah mountains, Marty had called me, and we had spoken about the possibility of reconciling our differences and making a fresh start.

Hours before I returned home in the late morning, Marty had come to take the three youngest of our seven children on an outing. He always loved a party and suggested they each bring a friend along.

So on that cold, January morning, they all crowded into his Suzuki XL-7 and drove sixty miles from our home in Bountiful to Honeyville for a day of winter water fun at the Hot Springs. In the meantime, I returned home and promptly went to bed to make up for the sleep I'd lost in exchange for visiting during the night.

Now as I drove to Honeyville, I prayed. *"Oh, please, Father, let Marty be okay so I can talk to him. Let me tell him the things I want to say."*

I mentally reviewed the little I knew: they'd been at the Hot Springs; Lucas had said "CPR"—maybe Marty had been in the water and stopped breathing. What had happened? What had he experienced? What had the children seen? What must they be going through right now?

Finally Lucas called back. "They're taking Dad to the hospital in Brigham City. Can Jared drive Dad's car and take us to the hospital?"

Oh yes, the car. Lucas didn't have his driver's license yet, and the children would all be stranded there at the resort. What else could I do? Jared was the only friend there old enough to drive. But he was young and hadn't had much driving experience, and besides, who could tell what emotional state he was in? On the other hand, what other option did they have? They were sixty miles away, and Marty was being taken in the ambulance.

"Yes. Just tell him to drive carefully."

"I will."

"Luke, can you tell me anything more about what happened?"

It seemed hard for him to talk, but after a moment he began. "I don't really know. We were swimming in the pool. Then we went down the slides a few times while Dad stayed in the pool. Well, the last time we went to the slides, when we came back, Dad was lying on the deck, surrounded by people, and someone was doing CPR on him."

Something in Lucas's voice had changed. He suddenly seemed so much older, and it frightened me. What was happening to our family?

"Luke, are you going to be okay? What about the kids?"

"I think we're okay. I hope you can come soon."

"I'm coming as fast as I can, honey. I love you, Luke."

"Bye, Mom. Love you too."

I called the older children who were away at George Wythe College in Cedar City, four hours south of home. Erin and Hillary, along with Anna and her husband Grant, all lived in the same apartment down there while attending school.

Erin answered. When I started to explain, she interrupted, asking, "Should we come up?"

I felt an urgency to gather the family. "Yes, honey, come as soon as possible."

I called Brooke, our oldest daughter in Logan, just over half an hour north beyond the hospital where they were taking Marty, and explained the situation. I heard a catch in her voice.

"Oh, no! I'll leave right now."

As I drove, I thought of others I needed to call. Who else needed to know Marty was in the hospital? My bishop. I tried his number, but there was no answer. I dialed again. Nothing. Panic began to rise in my chest, and I offered another prayer for strength.

Right away a thought came to my mind: *call Gayla.* From the day we'd moved into the neighborhood, Gayla had reached out to me and had been a friend on whom I could always depend. I dialed her number and heard her ever-cheerful voice. I had to consciously take a deep breath to be able to speak. Tears sprang to my eyes.

"Marty's being taken to the hospital in Brigham City . . ."

"Oh, Ros, what happened? Are you okay? What can I do to help?"

"I don't know what's happened. Lucas called but had to hang up, so I'm driving up, but I can't reach the bishop. Do you think you could contact him and the Relief Society President? Tell her I might not be there to play the piano at church tomorrow."

"No problem. I'll get hold of everyone. Drive safely. And Ros—don't worry. I'll be praying for you."

Just knowing she would be praying for me quieted my heart. I called my brother and sister, asking them to let the rest of the family know what was happening. I knew that the minute they all heard they, too would be offering prayers in our behalf. I called Marty's mother.

Just two years earlier, Marty's brother had died suddenly after heart surgery. His death had been extremely hard on her. I didn't want to worry her, but I felt she needed to know what was happening.

"Oh, Ros, no," she faltered.

"I'll call you as soon as I know anything more. Don't worry, Mom. I'm sure things will be okay."

I felt hypocritical telling her not to worry while my heart was pounding and my hands were trembling. I wondered if she sensed my desperation, and I prayed she hadn't. I wanted to protect her from any more pain if at all possible.

What I wanted most of all right now was not to have to be the strong one, but to have someone there to hold me and help me to think clearly. Since Marty had moved out, Lucas had been the one who offered that strength, but he was far away, and I felt weak and confused.

Why hadn't Lucas called by now? What could be taking so long?

Finally my cell phone rang.

"We're at the hospital now," Lucas told me. "And they've taken Dad into the emergency room."

"Did they give you any more information?"

"They didn't say anything. They just wheeled him in and closed the doors." He paused. "How soon will you be here?"

"I'm probably about twenty-five minutes away. Luke, can you call someone from Tremonton to come give Dad a blessing? Maybe Brother Christensen. See if he can find someone to bring with him."

Tremonton was a small town only minutes from Brigham City. It had been our home for twelve years, and we still kept in contact with many close friends there. Lucas agreed and hung up to make the calls.

As I drove, I felt surrounded by a dense fog; nothing was clear in my mind. My stomach grew tighter and tighter as I got closer to Brigham City. My hands were cold, and I wished I'd thought to grab some gloves as I'd left. I could barely focus on the road.

Can the other drivers have any idea what is happening? I wondered. *There they are, just driving casually to go shopping, or visiting, while I'm trying to get to the hospital where my husband is lying in the emergency room. Why does everyone drive so slowly?*

I was sure I was losing my sense of reality. The miles seemed to drag by, and every other car seemed to be moving in slow motion. It had never taken so long to drive this distance before.

Again, I prayed.

Help me, Father. Be near me. Calm my heart.

Finally, I reached the exit and headed toward the hospital, driving as fast as I dared.

As I turned into the hospital parking lot, it was almost as if I were watching myself from some other vantage point. I saw myself park the car, get out, and hurry toward the door. The experience was something out of a TV movie, not my life. I passed Marty's car parked next to the emergency entrance and the ambulance idling with the back doors still hanging open. A sudden pang twisted my heart. What would the next hours hold?

CHAPTER TWO

THE HOSPITAL

He stuns you by degrees—
Prepares your brittle Nature
For the ethereal Blow
By fainter Hammers—further heard—
Then nearer—then so slow
Your breath has time to straighten—
Your Brain—to bubble Cool—
Deals—One—imperial—Thunderbolt—
That scalps your naked Soul.

– EMILY DICKINSON –

I saw them as soon as the glare from the revolving glass door passed my eyes. There, out in the hallway near the doors to the emergency room, the children were huddled. I hurried over to them with my heart in my throat. Brooke had arrived shortly before me, and her face was tear-stained and sober; Meg was crying softly; Chris looked scared, and

7

Lucas looked deeply troubled. We embraced all together, saying nothing for a moment.

When I could find my voice, I asked, "Any word?"

They all just shook their heads. I wrapped my arms around Megan, rocking back and forth as I had when she'd been an infant. Lucas put his arms around us both and reassured me in a quiet voice.

"It's going to be okay, Mom. It's going to be okay."

I noticed their friends who'd been with them at the Hot Springs. They were gathered across the dimly lit hall. I went over, hugged each of them, and asked, "Are you okay?"

Immediately I wished I'd thought of something else to say. Of course they weren't okay. Their downcast eyes, their strained faces, were proof of their distress at the day's events. How awful for them to have been there while all of this was happening.

I wished their parents were there. "Would you like to call your parents on my cell?"

Jared answered, "No, thanks. We already called on the phone Luke has."

The phone Luke has? Oh, Marty's phone, I realized. My thoughts returned to Marty. *What is happening to Marty?*

I looked around the silent lobby for someone who I could ask about Marty. My eyes settled on the only visible hospital employee—the girl at the admitting desk—so I hurried over to her.

"How can I get information about my husband? He's in the emergency room."

"Are you Mrs. Reynolds?"

"Yes. How is he? Can I see him?"

"Come this way, please."

She led me through the swinging emergency room doors, then stopped me in the white-curtained foyer. A doctor and two EMTs stepped out from behind a curtain, careful to close it behind them, and introduced themselves briefly. I could hear movement still behind the curtain and longed to know what was happening.

"How is he? May I see him?" I asked, searching their faces.

"We're still working on him. We'll come for you as soon as we have some word. I'm sorry, but you'll need to wait outside."

Something in the way the EMT spoke made me feel weak and frightened. I couldn't read his expression—distant and hurried—and he dismissed me without another word, disappearing behind the curtain once more. Why had they let me come in this far but no farther? Couldn't I just *see* him?

I hung back as the receptionist guided me out through the doors, and before I could head over to the children she said, "I need to get the admitting information from you. Can you answer some questions for me?" I glanced over at the children, looking so alone and vulnerable, and back toward the emergency room doors. I felt torn. I wanted to be with the children, and I wanted to be in with Marty. I did *not* want to be answering questions—but I could see she expected me to comply.

"I guess so," I said, and followed her to the small cubicle where her computer stood on her desk, ready to take my information and add it to the hundreds of other names and numbers she must have typed into it in the past days and weeks. I sat in the black padded chair that was too low, feeling awkward and uncomfortable.

It was almost impossible to focus on what she was saying and asking me to do. My mind was so preoccupied with what might be going on in the emergency room and with the children back in the hall that I was nearly oblivious to all else. Once, the emergency room door opened and one of the EMTs whisked out past me, heading for the ambulance. I wanted to stop him and ask him about Marty, but he moved too quickly, and I couldn't get his attention.

With every passing minute, the dread in my heart grew. What could be taking so long? If there is no news by now, did it mean things were worse than we'd thought? Would there be brain damage? Would he be incapacitated for the rest of his life? How would his condition affect our life as a family?

Constantly, I prayed. *"Please, Father, let him be okay. Help me to accept Thy will—but if it's possible, let him be okay."*

The girl's voice pulled me back to the task at hand. "Mrs. Reynolds, excuse me, but do you have your insurance information? And your husband's employer's name?"

It seemed so absurd to be talking about such unimportant details when his life was hanging in the balance through the swinging doors to my left. I felt frustrated to have to be here giving numbers and dates to this girl who kept peering down at me with sympathy in her eyes. Finally I could bear it no longer.

"Couldn't I call in the rest of the information on Monday? I need to be with my children," I explained. She turned her gaze in their direction, hesitated, and finally agreed.

As I hurried over to where they were gathered, Paul, our neighbor from Tremonton, swung open the entrance doors with Jason, another of our old friends. Paul gave me a big hug.

After I explained what little I knew, they greeted each of the children; and then they approached the young lady at the admitting desk.

"Could we go in to Mr. Reynolds?"

She looked flustered. "I'm sorry, but you'll need to wait until the doctor comes out."

They leaned in closer, and in hushed voices asked something else. She shook her head, looked toward me, said a few more words, and the men turned away and walked back to rejoin us. Paul tenderly reached his arms around Megan and Chris, talking quietly to them, asking what had happened at the resort. Jason visited with Lucas, all the while keeping his eyes on the emergency room doors, waiting to be invited in.

Finally, the doors swung open and the doctor emerged. As he approached, I knew from his grim face that his news was not good. I tried to steel myself for whatever he had to say, but I felt my heart begin racing.

"Mrs. Reynolds?"

I tried to calm my voice. "Yes. How is he?"

"Could we meet in this room?" He directed me across the hall to the small, crowded office with a sign on the door that read, *Family Room*.

I swallowed hard and followed the doctor, motioning for the children to follow me. We silently filed in after him. Lucas and I stood next to each other, Brooke and Chris settled in the two chairs near the walls, and Brooke pulled Megan into her lap, wrapping her arms around Meg's shoulders. Paul and Jason stood in the doorway. All eyes were fastened on the doctor, who leaned against the desk, his shoulders slumped, his weary eyes making a circle around the room.

He paused a moment and then began. "We've attempted every possible procedure on Mr. Reynolds." He hesitated, and then began explaining the different procedures they'd tried: cardio-pulmonary resuscitation, defibrillation, and other terms completely foreign to me. My mind raced ahead of his words, dreading where they were leading.

"We've done all we can. There is nothing more we can do. He's not responding. I'm very sorry."

Not responding . . . nothing more we can do . . . did he mean . . . he hadn't said Marty had *died*. Was Marty comatose? What did the doctor mean?

He continued. "There's not much water in his lungs. We don't know if he had a heart attack or if he passed out in the water and then drowned. I'm so sorry."

I felt weak and leaned into Lucas's arms. I lifted my eyes and looked around the room at the children—some weeping quietly; all looking stunned.

The doctor reached for my hand, and his eyes searched mine. "I'm very sorry. I'll prepare him so you can go see him if you'd like. Then I'll need you to fill out some paperwork and answer a few questions. It shouldn't take too long." He excused himself and was gone.

Lucas wrapped his arms around me and held me close, while in my heart, I struggled to accept that this could really be happening.

The next hour at the hospital was the most difficult of my life. The children traveling from Cedar City had to be told. How I wished I could tell them when we were together so I could hold them close to soften the blow.

Erin answered her cell.

"Honey," I told her. "The doctor just came out, and . . . Daddy died."

I heard her gasp. Then, choking back tears, she relayed the message to the others. After a moment she asked, "Can we come to the hospital?"

"How close are you?"

"Probably a couple of hours."

"Well, I don't know how long we'll be here. Just keep driving, and I'll call you when we are finished here and ready to leave, and you can decide then."

She hung up, and my heart ached for the carload of our children, no longer anxious and worried, but now grieving and in shock.

I was so grateful for the men from our old neighborhood who had come. They hadn't been allowed in to give Marty a blessing, but now I asked them to give one to each of us. We closed the door of the *Family Room*, and a sweet spirit began to dispel the gloom and shock as each child received a blessing of comfort, peace, and strength to move forward through all that would now be necessary.

After the blessings, the nurse knocked on the door. "Anyone who would like to can now go in and see Mr. Reynolds."

I felt compelled to go. The fog settling in my mind was too thick—I had to see for myself this was real. My eyes swept the room—would any of the children want to go see him? Brooke shook her head, and Meg turned away, but Lucas and Chris nodded, and we turned to follow the nurse.

As we left the room, the bishop came through the hospital doors.

"Oh, bishop." I tried to say more, but it was several seconds before I could compose myself enough to tell him what he'd already guessed by my reaction—Marty had died. "We're going in to see him. Would you come?"

He nodded, and we turned toward the nurse.

She led the way down the hall through a different door and down a narrow hallway into the emergency room to a curtained area. As she pulled the curtain aside, I tried to prepare myself for what I would see, but when I saw Marty lying so still, the white sheet pulled up to his chest, my heart rebelled. It felt so *wrong*. I felt an unexpected anger rising in my heart—they'd given up too soon. But then I glanced around the room and saw all the signs of the exhaustive efforts at resuscitation—shock paddles, tubes, monitors—and remembered all the time we'd spent in the hall waiting while they worked on him, and into my heart swelled a confirmation of the doctor's words: "We've done all we could do."

I reached out for Marty's left hand; it was still warm. I wished I could speak to him just one more time, and I wondered how many of my thoughts he could be aware of now as I stood there, holding his hand. If only we could have spoken and reconciled. My heart ached as I pondered the many things I wanted to tell him. Mostly I wanted him to know I would always be grateful for every good thing that had come from our twenty-seven years of marriage. Why had I not told him when we were speaking the night before?

Fingering the wedding band on his hand, I pondered. *We didn't make much of a success of our marriage, and now there's no chance to heal the breach. Twenty-seven years ending like this. Why did it have to turn out this way?*

Whittier's words flew into my mind. *"Of all sad words of tongue or pen, The saddest are these: 'It might have been!'"*

So much "might have been," if only we'd had more years to work things out. If only things had been different. If only . . .

Everything began to blur in my mind. I felt faint and weak. It was too painful to be there. The bishop led me from the room into the hall, where the nurse told me I'd be introduced to the grief counselor. I'd never heard of one before, and as he came down the hall, I saw with surprise that he was wearing sandals, a T-shirt and jeans, and his long, silver-grey hair was braided down his back. I'd expected someone in a suit and tie. My first reactions were to wonder if he could relate to me, and how seriously he took his job.

He shook my hand, and introduced himself in a quiet voice. As he began to speak with me, I sensed his compassion and saw the genuine concern in his eyes, and I felt I could trust him.

As he began to lead me through the necessary paperwork, my mind was slow, and thinking was an effort. The doctor interrupted us to ask about an autopsy and organ donation. Having just been with Marty, holding his hand, I couldn't bear the thought of them doing anything to him. I declined. I just wanted them to leave him alone.

A chill swept over me when the counselor asked who I wanted to come and get "the body." I couldn't accept the fact that Marty wasn't "Marty" anymore—just "the body." Only then did I realize how providential it had been for Jason, one of the neighbors who had come, to be there: he was employed at the funeral home in Tremonton.

He was in the hall, talking with Lucas and Paul. I motioned to him to come near.

"Jason, would you . . . take Marty?" I could barely get the words out.

Tears filled his eyes, and he took my hand in his, pressing it firmly.

"Ros, I'd be honored."

As I watched him push open the doors to the emergency room, I could not imagine what families do when they don't know who will be taking the body of their loved one. How do they stand it? I could never have had a stranger take Marty. I was giving Jason a sacred trust, and I wept with gratitude that God had sent someone I knew to be the last person to take care of Marty.

It was over. I turned and saw all the children and my friends, the parents of the friends who'd been with our children, who had come, gathered in small groups in the hallway, quietly talking among themselves. One dear friend offered to take me in her car, but I declined. I wanted to be with my children. To my dismay, the three youngest had already arranged to ride home with their friends. I turned to Brooke.

"Will you ride with me?" I asked.

"Of course, Mom. I'll have someone take my car."

She asked one of my friends to drive her car to Bountiful, and we turned towards the exit. Brooke took my arm in hers. We both looked back towards the emergency room, then at one another, and walked out the doors.

As I left the hospital, my feet felt like dead weights. Each painful step seemed to widen and finalize the separation between Marty and me.

CHAPTER THREE

GATHERING

" . . . mourn with those that mourn,

and comfort those that stand in need of comfort . . ."

– MOSIAH 18:9 –

None of us had eaten since breakfast. We left the hospital in several cars, Brooke in the car with me, and the other children with different people who'd come to help. We formed a caravan, stopping at the drive-in across the street from the hospital before getting on the freeway for the hour-long drive home. I knew I should be hungry and asked for a small order of fries. As we paid at the window, I wondered what the cashier must think of us—somber, teary-eyed and withdrawn. How many carloads of people in that same condition did she see each week?

As we sat waiting for our food, I sensed a distance and resentment in Brooke.

"Brooke, what are you thinking?"

She looked over at me, her eyes filling anew with tears and her hands tightly clasping a tissue in her lap. She hesitated before speaking.

"Oh, Mom, I have a hard time believing that you are sad. I feel like your sorrow is all pretense. I know how you've been feeling about Dad. How can you cry now?"

It was like a slap in the face. I had been so absorbed in my own confusion and grief that I hadn't fully considered what the children must be feeling and thinking. What could I say to help her understand? How could I help her comprehend that, of course, I was grieving, not in spite of the separation, but even more *because* of it. Had Marty and I been together when he died, I would be grieving the loss of my sweetheart and my companion, tenderly aching for a future sweet reunion. But in my situation, I had already grieved for a long time as those feelings of oneness had been lost bit by bit over many years of difficulty, and through it all I had held out hope that through some miracle, someday that relationship could all be rebuilt. Now, with Marty gone, there was no hope for that. So in addition to mourning Marty's death, I was mourning what might have been but never would be; I was mourning the death of my dreams.

I tried to explain, and it came out clumsily. Brooke reached over, took my hand and held it in hers.

"I haven't understood how you've felt, and it's been so hard. I've hated this time with you and Dad being apart, and there in the hospital, I couldn't believe you were actually sad about this. Thanks for explaining, Mom . . . I *do* love you."

I remember so little of that drive. It was getting dark, and though we had spoken of caravanning home, I soon lost track of the other cars and drove on as if on auto-pilot. The pain in my heart and the jumble of thoughts in my mind preoccupied me.

When we arrived in Bountiful and approached the house, I could see cars in the driveway and recognized those of my brother and his wife, my sister and her husband, the friends who'd been at the hospital and neighbors who must have heard and wanted to do something to help.

I walked in the front door and was met by my brother. His eyes were red and his voice was unsteady.

"Hey, sis, I'm sorry." I melted into his hug, and for a few brief moments the tears that had been held at bay on the drive home finally found release. He touched my hair and lifted my chin so that our eyes met.

"What can I do?"

I felt weak, exhausted and confused. Just to have someone offering strength and security was such a support. Simply to feel his arms around my shoulders and to have someone answer all the questions, to help make decisions, and to notice when I needed to rest and make me lie down-—that was what I needed him to do. And throughout the next two days, he did.

We were soon surrounded by love. The house filled with people hugging us, crying with us, wanting to know what they could do. My mind was too numb to have answers.

"Just be here," was all I could say. People had already brought food—soup, rolls, pizza. Some of the children ate, but I had no appetite. All through the evening, as family, friends and neighbors dropped in, I drew strength from their hugs and their words of condolence and love, and I loved them for doing such an uncomfortable thing and coming over as soon as they heard. So many times I have heard of a tragedy in a family and thought, *I'll just pray for them. They probably don't want another person over there right now.* Yet here in our distress, each person that came and expressed love for us was a blessing to all of us.

We were standing in the crowded living room when we saw the carload of the rest of the children pull up into the circular driveway. They poured in the door, first Hillary, then Erin, Anna, and Grant, and as soon as they entered the house, the whole family gathered in one big group hug, and we could not hold back the tears. Our collective pain was indescribable, and none of us could speak. It was so hard to believe, and for those just arriving, even harder because they hadn't made it to the hospital. They had all so wanted to be able to see their dad, to speak to him at least one last time—and now, that chance was forever lost.

One by one our friends and extended family members left and the house settled into a numb quietness. We knelt in a halting, tearful family prayer and asked for strength for all that was ahead. Then, as the children settled into their beds, I worried about the youngest three. What must this day have been like for them? How would they ever recover from being so close to this tragedy? Would they feel responsible? Would they be blaming themselves? I wished I had taken the time to talk to them privately and see what they were feeling. Now it was too late, and I was too exhausted.

I had told Anna and Grant to take my room and sleep in the queen-sized bed. Hillary, Erin and Megan crowded in the middle room, and the boys were downstairs. Brooke and I slept in Meg's room on the day bed, Brooke on the top bed, I on the squeaky trundle that refused to pop up anymore. As I tried to fall asleep, things I should have said to Marty and things I should have done kept coming to mind. *If only I had . . .* prefaced every thought. After awhile, Brooke reached down and took my hand.

"It's okay, Mom. It's okay," she whispered. I hadn't realized I had been moaning as I tossed and turned, keeping her awake. She gently rubbed my hand as I tried to settle my mind. I was grateful to have her there, near me, and not to be alone on this night. I hoped for a blanket of forgetfulness to let my mind rest, and finally, sometime in the early morning hours, I fell asleep.

The next morning I awoke with aching eyes and a dull headache. I knew I needed to get up, but instead I curled up and drew the blankets closer around my shoulders to ward off the chill that had settled on our home during the night.

Suddenly I remembered that Jason would soon arrive to take care of all the burial arrangements, and I crawled out of bed, bracing myself against the chill in the air. I quickly slipped on my robe, trying to pull some warmth from the thick terry fabric, and stole out of the room and down the hall to turn up the heat and start getting ready.

The doorbell rang just as I was finishing, and I let Jason in and led him to the dining room table where we began discussing the burial plans. Several times during the process I had to shake myself to believe this was real. *Could I really be planning my husband's funeral?*

How is anyone supposed to choose a casket objectively at a time like that? Every sharp word of mine, every impatient action, every unkind thought ever directed at Marty—and we'd been married twenty-seven years—flooded my mind, and as they did, I couldn't bear the thought of letting money play a part in what casket I chose. I couldn't scrimp on the last thing I would do for him. I chose one made of a beautiful warm wood, with golden handles and corners.

We discussed the vault, the grave liner, the plot—all the necessary, awful details that have to be settled after a death. Jason sat patiently as I tried to blink away the fog that seemed to have taken up permanent residence in my mind. He carefully explained the pros and cons of each choice, and helped me to be as objective as possible. Decisions came slowly, but finally we completed the last of the forms.

Lastly, he explained the process for the viewings and funeral. Brooke had been standing behind my chair, running her hands through my hair as we talked. Jason looked over the funeral planning sheet and said,

"Your family can plan the funeral completely on your own if you'd like to."

I looked up at Brooke, wondering if we were up to that, and she nodded.

"Okay, we'll do it."

Jason handed me the general outline for funerals and gathered his things. I walked him to the door, and as he opened it, he asked, "Do you have any more questions?"

"No, you've been so good to explain it all. How can I thank you, Jason?"

"I'm honored to help you. Marty was a good friend."

He turned and walked through the falling snow to his truck.

I gathered the children to the living room to discuss the funeral plans.

"Who wants to be part of it?"

There was a pause, and Brooke led out. "I'll speak."

"Are you sure, honey?"

"Yes. I want to do it, Mom."

"Okay. Anyone else?"

Lucas looked up.

"I'll play my guitar. Do you think Uncle Clive would play with me? We could do *Romanza*. Dad liked that."

"I'm sure Clive would love to. Why don't you call him?"

Lucas left to make the call, and I looked at Megan. From the time she was tiny, she was always singing around the house, and Marty loved to hear her. He'd do almost anything to persuade her to sing in public. He loved to see his children perform.

"Meg, would you want to sing?"

She looked up at me, hesitating.

"You don't have to, honey. I know Daddy would love it, but I totally understand if you don't think you could do it."

"No, Mom, it's okay. I'll do it."

She started getting teary-eyed, and I gave her a hug.

"You'll do beautifully. I know you will. Why don't you choose one of your favorite Primary songs, and we'll put it on the program. Maybe Beverly would accompany you."

"Would you call her, Mom?"

I agreed. Beverly had been the children's piano teacher ever since we'd moved to Bountiful, and I knew if she was available, she'd play for Meg.

"I'll read the life sketch," Hillary volunteered.

"Well that looks like everything we need. Chris, Erin, Anna, is there anything you'd like to do?"

They shook their heads, then Grant offered,

"I'll make a video montage."

I hadn't even thought of one—I have no skills in that area, but Grant is an experienced videographer, and I was grateful we would have something of a professional quality to show honoring Marty's life at the viewings.

Erin spoke up. "We can help him find pictures and music. There's nothing else we need on the program is there?"

We had asked Marty's brother Don to speak, and his close friend Jim, and had chosen the invocation and benediction. We didn't really want a long service.

"No. That completes the list Jason gave us. I'll call this in to him."

That evening was a blur. I know many friends and family came and went, but it's all hazy in my memory. One thing is clear, however: I remember feeling an outpouring of love and concern that engulfed our home. That night in our family prayer, I remember thanking God that we lived where we did, surrounded by so many compassionate, loving people who were doing so much to bear us up.

CHAPTER FOUR

FAREWELL

"You must do the thing you think you cannot do."

— ELEANOR ROOSEVELT —

I lay in the early-morning silence, and one thought kept going through my mind: "*We should go be with Marty.*"

Jason had offered to let us come have some private time with Marty before the viewings and funeral, but it was a seventy-five mile drive up to the mortuary in Tremonton where Marty was, and I just couldn't see a time when we could fit that in.

I pulled the blankets more tightly around my shoulders as I argued with myself.

"*What if the children don't want to? What if they're uncomfortable when I propose it? What will I say to them?*"

However, the desire to go see him only grew stronger with each passing moment, and I decided to call Jason.

"Ros, if you can come up this evening, I'll stay open for you, and you can spend some time with him alone."

I felt compelled to be near Marty, so I arranged to meet Jason at the funeral home at 6:00 that night.

I hung up and wondered how the children would feel about that decision. At breakfast I announced that we were going. I didn't ask them if they wanted to go; I just stated that we would.

"Why, Mom?"

It was Megan. I knew it would be uncomfortable for her. Actually, it would probably be uncomfortable for us all, but I felt strongly we all needed to be there.

"I just feel we need to do this, honey. We won't stay too long, and we'll go to dinner afterwards at El Asadero."

Erin had worked at the small Mexican restaurant in town when we'd lived in Tremonton, and we all had fun memories of the few times we'd gone there for dinner just so Marty could leave her a big tip.

The rest of the children accepted the idea without complaint, though I sensed some of them were simply 'humoring Mom.'

After setting a time to leave that afternoon, I left with the girls to choose a burial plot at the cemetery. My mother had offered me one of the plots next to my father and infant brother. I wondered as we walked there, just how much of this life those who have gone on before us are aware of. Was Dad there, watching me? Did he know all that had transpired?

Dad had suffered a stroke that had left him bedridden and unable to communicate for almost ten years. But he could listen. Many were the times that I had gone and visited him, telling him of my struggles and concerns. Not able to speak, he would just hold my hand and squeeze it for a response. I remember one difficult day laying my head on his chest, weeping with despair at the shambles of my marriage and feeling his hand gently stroking my hair. When I raised my eyes to look up at him, tears were rolling down his cheeks.

Since his death, in my darkest hours I had sometimes felt him near me, and I wondered, could he see me now?

I chose a plot near his, finished the arrangements at the cemetery and drove to Dillard's to meet Gayla, who had insisted on buying me a new outfit for the viewings and funeral. The girls hadn't brought dresses up from Cedar City, so I had them purchase something to wear, too.

I hugged Gayla as she handed me the bag holding the new clothes, and as she turned to leave, she said, "Thanks for allowing me to do this!"

I walked to the car with the girls, marveling at the tender mercies God was showering down upon us through the people He had brought into my life.

When we reached home, I rested for a few minutes until it was time to get ready to go. Bishop Rasband had lent us his fifteen-passenger van allowing all of us to drive together in one vehicle, so I gathered the family and we all piled in.

I was worried about what the children would be feeling about this trip, but Grant and Erin both had their new laptops with them, and all the other children were watching as they talked about and demonstrated different applications and games on the computers. There was a general light-heartedness in the van, and it calmed my heart. I thought, "This won't be so bad. We'll be fine."

However, as we approached Brigham City, I dreaded driving past the area the children had last seen Marty alive and the hospital where we had left him. The noise in the van became quieter and I wondered what all the children were thinking. I could see in my rear-view mirror that some were resting, some were focused on the computer screens, and some were gazing out the window, deep in thought. I felt awkward, and as we neared Tremonton, I wondered if this was an unwise venture. Would I regret taking the children? Would they be uncomfortable—even upset that I had brought them? Would they even want to see Marty?

Night had fallen while we traveled. As we drove up to the funeral home, it was aglow with lights, and through the open door amber light was streaming out onto the snow-lined sidewalk. I climbed down from the van and approached the door, noticing that a few of the children were hanging back, and in my heart I prayed,

"Please, Father, help them feel peace here. Help them to accept what has happened, and to find here what each of them needs, whatever that may be."

Jason greeted us at the door. "Marty is in this room," he motioned as he walked toward the nearest room. "Feel free to take all the time that you need. I'll wait out here."

We entered, hesitating, and looked across the large room to the far side where the casket stood in a small recessed area. The lamplight shed a soft light on the cream-colored carpet and the elegant furnishings. All was still and silent, and it felt to me as if we were entering a sanctuary.

As we crossed the room, the children instinctively slowed and drew near to each other, and as we walked up to the open casket, without even thinking our arms entwined and we came together in a semi-circle around Marty, weeping. A lifetime of memories, regrets, and unfulfilled dreams all flooded into my mind. Why had it ended this way? Why couldn't he have lived just long enough for each of us to be able to say goodbye and thank him for the good he had brought into our lives?

As the sobs subsided and we could find our voices again, we spoke of how good he looked, and how beautiful the casket was, and how peaceful it felt there. A calm seemed to rest upon us as we gathered there, gazing in at him, so near and yet an eternity away.

The north door of the mortuary near the casket area opened, and in walked the owner of the funeral home. President Ward Taylor had been our bishop, our stake president and dear friend while we had lived in Tremonton. He took me in his arms, and I could not contain my emotions. I wept freely, and he tenderly, patiently held me. I felt like I was in my Heavenly Father's arms as he comforted me.

"Oh, Ros. I know, I know. It hurts. And that's a good sign. There'd be something wrong if we didn't hurt."

The children were weeping too, and he moved around to each one, hugging and comforting them in turn. He reminisced about Marty, sharing anecdotes from the past and stories that made us laugh.

He stayed quite awhile, offering reassurance and solace. I didn't ever want him to leave; I felt stronger when he was near. But he stepped back, looked around at each of us, and said,

"You know, you're a great family. I sure love you." Then he assured us he would see us in Bountiful the next afternoon, excused himself and left.

His coming was another of God's tender mercies. I felt like a shaft of light had descended on us all and brought comfort and hope and the beginnings of healing.

One by one the children turned away from the casket, and I felt it was time to go. I looked one last time at Marty, then turned and walked into the other room.

"Jason, thank you. We needed this."

"You're very welcome, Ros. I was glad to do it. "

He asked what our plans were for the rest of the evening.

"We're going to El Asadero for dinner, then we'll head home."

He smiled and reached out to shake my hand.

"Good idea," he said and bid us goodbye.

After we'd been seated at the table in the restaurant, the children spoke of President Taylor's visit and laughed again at some of the things he'd mentioned. We spoke of some of our humorous memories of Marty, and it felt so good to be all together, and to be able to smile for a few moments.

During the meal, to our surprise Jason walked in. He'd brought his daughter with whom Megan had spent much of her time when we were neighbors. The two girls hugged and visited for a few minutes, Jason cautioned us about the road conditions on the way home, told us to drive carefully, and they left.

We finished and I stepped to the cash register. The cashier smiled at me and said,

"It's been paid."

I know I looked confused, and she repeated, "An anonymous person paid your bill for you."

We never found out who provided that meal for us. Was it Jason? Dennis, Brooke's boyfriend from Logan had joined us for dinner and had left the table for a moment in the middle of the meal. A family that we knew from our years living in Tremonton was eating when we arrived, and we had exchanged greetings. It could have been any of them, or someone else. We will never know who paid our tab. It's hard to describe how that generous act touched our hearts. We all came away filled with gratitude, humility, and a desire to be more like the people who lifted our burdens that day.

My father was second youngest in a large family. Through my youth, we attended several viewings for grandparents, and then for aunts and uncles—Dad's elderly brothers and sisters as they passed on in their old age. To me viewings were peaceful, loving gatherings—more celebrations of great lives well-lived than anything else. Yes, there were tears of fond remembrance, and a sense of sorrow at not having that person near anymore, but the overall feeling was one of peace.

Now I wondered what the viewings for Marty would be like. Everything was different this time. Would there be any peace for me or the children?

The day was filled with preparations, and it passed quickly. All too soon we were at the door of the mortuary.

The heavy door swung open revealing thick carpeting in the hall, beautiful woodwork on the walls, and ornate carving on the crown molding next to the ceiling. A deep silence reigned, and a feeling of awe came over us all as we entered and walked down the hall looking for someone who could direct us. Brooke walked ahead of us, and as she turned to enter the first open doorway, she gasped—and began to sob.

As we each reached the doorway, we understood why. We all were stunned by the sight of the open casket and by the profusion of flowers filling the room. We were touched deeply, and not one of us could speak as our eyes traversed the room and we saw evidence of how many people had been touched by Marty's life and had wanted to express their love for him.

The children made several trips to the car, bringing in the items we had gathered from the house that would best show Marty's personality and the things he loved. A fly-fishing pole, some of the photos he'd taken, his French dictionary, a smattering of *things* attempting to sum up a mortal life.

Once the displays were set up and Grant had started the video, President Taylor gathered us around the casket and addressed the children.

"You know life is going to be different without your dad here. But he's not that far away. Remember how near the spirit world is, and that your dad can still be part of your life. When you need him, you can feel him near you, and he can be cheering you on as you strive to make those choices that will enable you to be with him again. Your dad was a good man. Live to honor and bring joy to him."

He spoke on, teaching us of the Atonement and how it allows us to change and grow, to heal and have hope. He reminded us of the Savior's promise never to leave us comfortless, and of His saving grace.

He finished and stepped to the side of the casket. We all moved closer and gazed in at Marty. Arms lifted to embrace shoulders, hands linked and clasped, and we stood silently, pondering all we had heard.

A sound from the back of the room broke the reverie. We turned to see people signing the guest book, and President Taylor gave us last-minute instructions and tips on the protocol of viewings.

"From the amount of flowers, I imagine there will be a lot of people.

We'll need to help the line move along the best we can. No life stories exchanged tonight," he said with a smile and a twinkle in his eye.

He was right. Once the line began, we had a steady stream of people. We didn't have time for life stories—or even to catch up as much as I would have liked to. Family came from near and far. Friends came from Bountiful, Tremonton, and from Taylorsville where we had lived twenty years earlier. Professionals and associates from Marty's work were there.

I drew great solace from the people coming through the line. Their words and their hugs lifted me and encouraged me. It touched me that so many had given up their evening to come offer their love and condolences. I never wanted it to end. The love and support and comfort I felt were incredible.

The same was true of the viewing the next morning. Again I was astonished at the number of people who came, and I was touched by their love and respect for Marty. I was repeatedly grateful for the thought that he might be permitted to be present and that he might be able to know he had left such a positive imprint on this world in his life. I kept thinking, *"What a tribute to his life."*

His employer came through the line with his wife, and we all wept together. They had been good friends with us, and in their embrace I also sensed that with Marty gone, my relationship with them would be changing. Bit by bit the realization was forming that my life was about to change in more ways than I could ever have imagined.

The viewing was over so fast that I felt incredulous. Could the time have passed that quickly? I saw President Taylor and Jason closing the doors to the room; the talking quieted, and people turned and faced President Taylor as he addressed us.

"We invite you to join us now as Lucas offers the family prayer."

Heads bowed, and Lucas' voice filled the room, emotional but steady, and the prayer was tender and full of truth. As he continued, muffled weeping could be heard around the room.

He closed and President Taylor spoke. "We invite all who would like to come say their final goodbyes to move up to the casket at this time."

I stood aside, letting Marty's siblings and his mother approach first. I saw the pain on their faces, every move betraying sorrow and heartache.

Our children approached next. I felt deep sadness as I looked at each of their faces and saw the trauma and disbelief, and as I heard their sobs. Through my mind flashed future scenes: no daddy-daughter dates ever again; no father at their weddings; no grandpa bouncing their children on his knee; no dad at the father-son campouts. No Dad.

I drew near and looked at Marty. My heart was so heavy. I so wanted to have made peace between us, to have reached an understanding and brought closure to the trials we had been through. If only we could have been reconciled before he left this life.

I laid my hand on his hands. They were cold. His face looked so healthy and peaceful, as if he were just in a deep sleep. I would have preferred our last moments to be private. I wanted to be able to linger with him there, and talk to him, but I felt awkward being surrounded with so many people.

Finally President Taylor asked, "Are you ready?"

I nodded, stepped back, and my gaze froze on President Taylor's hands as they turned the handle that lowered Marty's body in the casket and then closed the lid. Everything seemed to move into slow motion, and the reality of it all hit me with piercing clarity. Our time with Marty in this sphere was over.

PART TWO

THE BEGINNING

Chapter Five

Grieve!

Will I ever wake up without weeping?

I began to wonder after several days what life was going to be like now. *Is this what it's like to be a widow—a heart that feels like a dead weight; a mind that refuses to function clearly, perpetually living in a fog and being unreliable when decisions loom; confusion about the simplest tasks; and tears—unbidden, sudden and recurring tears?*

I once heard a story of a pioneer sent to colonize a remote area where eking out an existence required back-breaking work in the river bottoms, day after day. The man's diary entry every night for months on end read as follows: "Grubbing in the bottoms."

Working through grief felt like that. I woke up, I dressed, I did the necessary tasks of the day, and I went to bed. Grubbing. Just forcing myself to put one foot in front of the other and keep going for one more day.

While grieving, life can feel unfamiliar, unsettled, and uncomfortable—even unwanted. Questioning one's sanity can be a common, daily occurrence. And though each person's grief is unique, understanding the commonalities and the usual phases of the process can make a world of difference in the experience of mourning.

It was helpful to me to learn that there is an actual process to grieving, with clear, definable steps, although each person goes through those steps in their own order and at their own pace, and the steps seem anything but clear while one is passing through them. Some steps people even go through repeatedly, but eventually each phase is worked through, and healing can come. Grief can be survived and even recovered from, and although one never "gets over" a death, one *can* learn to simply *live on*.

Just what is the process of grief, and why do we fear and avoid it?

According to Webster, grief is "intense emotional suffering caused by loss."[1] Author Deanna Edwards says, "Grief is our emotional, physical, spiritual, and intellectual response to loss. It is the overwhelming involvement of all of our senses to deprivation."[2]

"The overwhelming involvement of all of our senses."

Those who have grieved know how accurate that description is. Grieving is extremely painful, physically and emotionally, and there are very few humans who want to experience pain voluntarily. The natural tendency is to avoid pain at all costs. So some choose to ignore the grieving process, to push down the emotions when they threaten to surface, and to stoically push ahead with life, insisting that they are fine.

Yet we must consciously decide to experience the entire grieving process if we are to heal fully. Just as a traumatic wound, in order to heal, needs to be cleaned out, broken bones set, and tissue sutured—all things involving additional pain after the injury—so in emotional trauma the healing process must begin, in Deanna Edwards' words, "from the inside out, or the wound will become infected and leave a permanent scar."[3]

---

1 *New World Dictionary of American English Third College Edition, 1988* Simon & Schuster, Inc. p.593

2 *Grieving, The Pain and the Promise,* Deanna Edwards, Covenant Communications, Inc. American Fork, Utah 1989, p.3

3 *Grieving, The Pain and the Promise,* Deanna Edwards, Covenant Communications, Inc. American Fork, Utah 1989, p.114

There are those bearing such scars around us even now. One woman told me of her friend whose wife was prescribed a medication that reacted violently with one she was already taking. Within hours of taking the drug, she was dead. Her husband could never accept her death, nor find purpose in life anymore, and after years of living in depression and isolation, he finally took his own life.

It needn't be that way. We can take a different path. It will involve knowing the process of grieving and being willing to work through each step.

I'll give here a brief list of the steps in the grieving process, then later I will discuss each step in detail.

Shock—One feels stunned and finds it difficult to grasp what has happened. Emotionally it can feel like a "slap in the face."

Denial—One simply cannot accept that the death has occurred. Unrealistic expectation fill one's mind, ("maybe he will be okay; maybe they are wrong") and one attempts to function in the illusory dream of what they wish were true.

Numbness—Unable to feel any emotion, one just goes through the necessary motions to get through the day like an automaton. C. S. Lewis described it as having an invisible blanket between the world and oneself. This numbness has been described as nature's way of buffering the deep pain until we are more ready to handle it. Some people choose to stay in this stage, preferring numbness to the possibility of future pain.

Confusion—One feels like they could be losing their mind. Thoughts are disorganized, forgetfulness sets in, and the ability to concentrate is limited. Decisions seem innumerable and impossible to make.

Emotional Release—Sudden tears set off for no apparent reason and with no warning are common. One feels completely out of control of his or her emotions.

Anger—This can be felt towards the person who died: "Why did he leave me?" or at others: "Why didn't they do more to help?" "How could that driver not have seen him?" or at God: "Why didn't He prevent this?"

Guilt—A very common reaction where one asks, "Why didn't I . . ." or "If only I had . . ." This guilt can be especially difficult to avoid when the surviving spouse feels the death could have been avoided if they had done something differently.

Depression and Isolation—Others don't seem to understand, and one feels alone in sorrow. Being around others is difficult, and being alone is easier than trying to socialize and pretend to be happy. Anger turned inward, rather than expressed, can create or increase this depression. A heavy sadness permeates life, and one feels empty. There can seem to be no reason to go on, no purpose in life.

Recovery and acceptance—The definition of recovery is going to be different for each person. You have to decide what it means for you. Expecting the tragedy to be erased and never affect you again is unrealistic. But you can expect to get to a point where the tragedy doesn't define your life, where you can find happiness and peace, and live a full life again.

Most people go through each of these steps, sometimes more than once, before reaching the place where they feel like they can move ahead with life. I went through some stages fairly quickly; others I still see manifested in my life. Confusion sometimes rears its head, and emotional release will still reduce me to tears at unexpected moments.

What can be done to ease the passage through these phases? How can we approach each one so we can achieve the most complete healing?

SHOCK

Debbie's husband, a healthy man, went to work Friday morning. At 4:21 that afternoon, Debbie received a call that her husband had been found in the copy room, unresponsive, not breathing, and that the paramedics were there. They were never able to resuscitate him.

When I asked Debbie what got her through those first hours, she said, "Hands down, what helped most was prayer. I would look up to the sky and pray to God that he would give me the strength to live for ten minutes, then ten more minutes, and then ten more, until after a few hours I was able to extend my prayers to hours instead. As I prayed, I could feel the arms of God wrap around me and comfort me."

In addition to prayer, it is important to have people near at this time who can help you think, hold you, feed you, and care for you while you are struggling to realize what has happened. This shock is more than an emotional reaction; it is physical too, and you need to be aware of your physical needs during those first hours and days. Eat (although you may have no desire for food,) rest whenever you get a chance, and keep taking fluids. Dehydration can create many of the same symptoms as depression, and it is vital to keep hydrated when dealing with shock.

DENIAL

Anne's husband collapsed suddenly while the two of them were on vacation at a resort. Paramedics took him to a nearby hospital. While Anne sat outside the emergency room, she planned all she would talk to her husband about as soon as she could see him, and about the things they would do when he was released from the hospital. When the doctor told her he had died, she just knew he was wrong.

"I wanted to tell him, "Go back in there. You have stopped too soon. He is going to live!"

Many women find themselves thinking, "This isn't real. This can't have happened. It's all a bad dream and I'll wake up soon." Only after the hours pass and the necessary tasks force a widow to admit *this is real* will the reality begin to settle. Know that you may feel these unreasonable feelings and think illogical thoughts. Don't beat yourself up over it, or be ashamed; it's a natural reaction. The only problem comes when one continues to live in denial, refuses to admit what has happened, and resists moving on with life.

NUMBNESS

Oh, the blessed days of numbness! Realize that while your emotions are subdued, you have a window of time to adjust to your loss. Use these days to allow yourself to rest, to begin to realize what life will be like now, and to care for yourself. Don't force things – spend your time connecting with loved ones, accepting their offerings of love, and save your energy for the next steps in your healing process. Trust that your emotions will return, and you *will* feel again if you allow it. Determine now to welcome your emotions when they return, knowing that they will be the key to healing and to a meaningful life in the future.

CONFUSION

Yvonne's husband suffered for over twelve years as cancer and other diseases took their toll on his body. Three nights before he died, the discomfort he was in turned to real pain, and he was put on morphine. He slept in his recliner, and she slept next to him on the couch. One night she awoke at about 2:00 a.m. and listened to his breathing. She was very wide-awake, so she got up and went and touched him. She wrote of that early morning:

"He felt a bit clammy so I got a bowl of warm water and a flannel and washed him down and dried him and made him as comfortable as possible. I went into the kitchen and made a warm drink, came back into the sitting room and sat down beside him."

"I took hold of his hand and said, "Wally, I do love you, darling." He squeezed my hand, took a breath and died. He just ceased to breathe."

Although she had known for years this day would come and knew it would happen, she was still profoundly affected by his death. Thinking clearly was a struggle. She later wrote:

"When you suffer a traumatic loss, your brain doesn't work properly."

Most widows would agree this is, at best, an understatement. My brother met me at the door of my home as I returned from the hospital, and he helped me through those first hours. I remember being asked questions and looking with a blank stare at him, wondering what had just been said. There were moments when I simply could not process information. This stage is where having support is especially important. There are so many decisions that have to be made. If you are confronted with choices that can be put off until later, do so. Focus on the vital, immediate decisions. When you feel clouded by confusion, it is helpful to find someone with a clear head with whom you can discuss your options. Just being able to talk through them can help you see more clearly. Know this will pass, and clarity does return.

EMOTIONAL RELEASE

Linda wrote, "I would break down at the grocery store, at school, and other places. It seemed like every time I started to get some control, someone would say something and I would break down and cry all over again. Everything seemed to make me cry."

I met Suzie at a training session. As we introduced ourselves and realized we were both widows of nearly three years, I asked her how she was doing.

She paused, swallowed, and tears filled her eyes. She couldn't speak, excused herself and left the room. Later she apologized, explaining that she could never account for what would make that happen. She felt vulnerable whenever she left home, never knowing when she would be overcome by some casual remark.

I have experienced the same thing. Months after the funeral I would be out running errands, and for no particular reason, I would feel the sobs coming. I learned that one of the most important things to be done at this point is to allow them to come.

Growing up I thought that emotions were something to be controlled, ignored, or buried. Only as I read more about grief and mourning did I come to understand that emotions are part of this human experience. They are part of what makes us each who we are. Feeling them, acknowledging them, and living through them helps us to be more human, and makes us more able to empathize with our fellow human beings.

I got to the point where, when I felt the sadness descending, rather than trying to stop the feelings, wherever I was, I would find a way to take time to release them. If I was driving, I would pull over as soon as I could, and simply cry until I was done. If I was at home, I would go into my room and pour out my heart. At first, it was as if each time I was pulling emotions from deeper and deeper in my soul, and it was physically very painful. I wondered if I would ever be free from that profound ache. But as time went on, the sobs came less frequently and were more fleeting, and my heart was lighter after each occurrence.

Allowing these emotions to surface and to be fully felt, and acknowledging the trauma you have been through, actually helps the healing process along. It has been said that tears are God's way to let the pain out. Accept them as cleansing; allow them to flow, and release them. Each time you do, you are releasing the pain and trauma and promoting the renewal of your soul.

ANGER

"How dare he leave me? He knew I couldn't make it alone. I can't believe he did this to me," Maria lamented to her neighbor after her husband's death. All through their marriage, she had always said to him, "You are so much a part of my life, I could never live without you." Then he was found on the floor at his office, a victim of a fatal heart attack.

Now she felt anger that he had 'left' her to live her life alone.

Rosa was angry at the drunk driver who took her husband's life. "How can I look at her and not be angry?" she asked her pastor. They had left home for a quick errand, leaving the children alone "for just a few minutes." Rosa never even saw the car that hit them, and hours later she had awakened in the hospital to learn that her husband had been killed instantly in the crash that had left her with injuries that would take months to recover from.

"How could God ask me to go through this?" Angela wonders. She feels that God could have answered her prayers for healing for her husband, yet instead he died. His pancreatic cancer had been diagnosed only months before, and it had taken him quickly and cruelly. Watching her husband die a painful death had been excruciating for her.

Feeling anger after a death or tragedy is common, even for those who normally don't get angry. Leisa told me, "I thought I was wrong to feel angry—that I would be a bad person if I felt anger. But it was only after I allowed myself to admit that I was angry and expressed those emotions and dealt with them, that I could move on and begin to heal."

Write out your angry feelings to get them on paper and then let them rest there. Pray for help to be free from them. As you release these feelings, you pave the way for your future healing

GUILT

"If only I had gone with him." "Why didn't I tell him I loved him when he left this morning?" "If only I had taken better care of him, he wouldn't have died."

One must determine to be tender with oneself here. The past is past, and these questions can only do harm. As you walk the difficult path of grief, determine to replace them with questions such as, "What can I learn from this moment?" "What can I do today to make a difference for good?" "What would God have me do next?"

Depression and Isolation

"I can't even get out of bed. Everything is darkness now."

"I can't go out anywhere. People expect me to be cheerful, and I can't be. Nobody understands, and they all think I should be better by now. I just want to stay at home."

"I wish people would just leave me alone. No one can fix this, and I wish they'd stop trying."

Darkness. We have all felt it. But when it persists, it can become overwhelming. There are steps we can take to help move toward the light, and learning about them can help restore hope, one step at a time. Share your struggles with a friend who has grieved and who can help you through this challenging time. Hold on and know that healing can come. You can once more feel hopeful; you can once again feel comfortable mingling with humanity; but it will take time, and you will need a desire to learn and grow.

As I have visited with other women who have grieved, I find those who are experiencing the greatest healing have learned these steps and recognize them, acknowledging they are part of the healing process and, therefore, accepting that as the stages come, they must be lived through and *felt* before they can be dismissed.

One tendency is to refuse to grieve—to become numb emotionally in an effort to avoid being hurt any further. However, being numb works both ways—it prevents pain, but it also prevents profound joy. Choosing not to feel is also a choice not to live fully.

As Rabbi Earl A. Grollman, Ph.D. said, "In our innumerable efforts to escape from pain, we also escape the wonders of love . . . Were it not for the grief of a love lost, our humanity, in its deepest sense would not exist. Darkness and light, joy and anguish, are strands in the texture of life. The season of grief is the prelude to new meaning and new life."[4]

4 *Grieving, The Pain and the Promise*, Deanna Edwards, Covenant Communications, Inc. American Fork, Utah 1989, Forward by Rabbi Earl A. Grollman

The journey though grief, though painful, is one of self-discovery. It is an opportunity to grow and move on to a deeper appreciation of all that comprises this journey we call life.

ESSENTIAL TASKS FOR GRIEVING

- Grieve! Determine to allow the grief to come. Cry when you feel like it. Feel the pain; don't stop it. As you suffer, believe it is cleansing your heart and soul and releasing the hurt so you can eventually heal.

- Go to SistersInHope.com and check out the section "First Steps When Tragedy Strikes." Use the suggestions there to help you keep focused during the first days and weeks.

- Learn all you can about grief. Check out the references in the appendix. Become an educated traveler on this pathway you now tread.

- Read the next six chapters and put into practice all that rings true to you.

- Be patient. Know that grief can take a long time to run its course. The best thing to do is to accept that fact and not try to rush your healing. No matter what anyone else says, you are the only one who knows your timetable. Grieve, knowing this process is leading to a better place than where you are now.

CHAPTER SIX

FIND FRIENDS

"Oh, the comfort, the inexpressible comfort of feeling safe with
a person, having neither to weigh thoughts nor measure words,
but pouring them all out, just as they are, chaff and grain together,
certain that a faithful hand will take and sift them, keep what is
worth keeping, and with a breath of kindness blow the rest away."

– DINAH CRAIK (1826-1887) –

"Hi, Ros. It's Sue."

My heart filled with gratitude, and tears sprang to my eyes. How did she know I needed to hear her voice just then?

"Oh, Sue—"

"Are you okay?"

When I could speak again, I answered, "Well, you know how it is."

She did. Her husband had lost his battle with a long-term illness five years before. She'd walked this path and knew it well. When she came through the line at the funeral a week ago, she told me she'd be calling me. I was surprised—and grateful—that she'd called so soon.

"Can I come up someday this week? I'd like to help you get the Social Security payments set up for the children and show you some things that helped me get things in order."

We set a time, and very soon she was sitting at my dining room table. She had brought homemade soup, and just the aroma of the herbs steeping with vegetables piqued my appetite; I felt the unfamiliar pang of hunger. It was good to feel a desire to eat again. As we shared that meal and talked, I felt nourished physically and emotionally. Her tender words lifted my aching heart, and it felt so liberating to be able to say whatever I was feeling, without having to measure my words or be afraid of the tears that would spring up without any warning. Sue understood.

After lunch, we went through the financial paperwork. What I'd gathered was dismally insufficient. I had attempted to find everything we would need, but often as she asked for a document or file, I realized I'd forgotten that one, and the cloud of shame and confusion would begin to engulf me. Sue immediately offered words of encouragement.

"Don't worry about it today. There's time. We'll get this all together. It just takes time. No worries!"

We made a list of paperwork to find, and Sue made a call to the Social Security office. Her sister worked there, and with her help, we were able to get an appointment set up for the very next week. We went over a few other things, and when it was time for Sue to leave, she gave me a hug, opened the door, and then as the cold air blew in, she turned to me.

"If it's all right, I'll be back next week at the same time. We can go over your finances, or whatever would be helpful. You decide. I'll just plan on being here—and I'll bring lunch again!"

Sue was true to her word. For weeks I could count on her being there one day each week, helping me sort through the maze of financial paperwork and legal issues I needed to face. She gave me the names of her health and life insurance agents so I could compare quotes and ask questions, and she helped me set up a filing system for my paperwork similar to the one she used. Probably the most valuable thing about her coming was she was someone I could be "real" with. Whenever my emotions overcame me, she took me in her arms and held me until the torrent ended. Then, with her knowing smile, she'd ask if I was ready to continue, and we'd move on, together, doing what I could not do on my own.

When we grieve, we need a friend who will support us, affirm our value, and be there when we question our sanity. When you're going through the dark times, a friend can be the difference between despair and hope.

Who that friend is may change as you go through your healing. Sue was there for those first months, and then gradually our times together became less and less frequent. Then another friend stepped in, as if on cue, and filled another need. It seemed as if each time I had a need and prayed for help, a friend appeared who was perfect for my need.

Multiple friends have helped me, but usually they come into my life one at a time and sometimes from unexpected sources. Sometimes the help has come from a complete stranger; other times, as with Sue, it has been a friend I've known for years.

What if you can't think of even one person who you could feel close enough to open up to? How do you find the support you need?

Think through your family, extended family, and circle of friends. Consider those you know through your church. Who do you know who has grieved before? Pray to know who your friend could be for that time. God knows your need, and He knows the people who can be the most helpful to you at each stage of your grief. Pray that you will be open to whomever it is, and to be led to them when the time is right. Consider those you have noticed who are compassionate, patient, and open to friendship. Then make a call, start a conversation, send an email—anything to start the process of making a new friend.

There are many widows' groups and loss groups, both locally and online. A list of some national organizations is found in the appendix. Some widows have told me that the group has been their lifeline. On the other hand, sometimes the very best option is just one friend in whom you can develop trust and confidence, someone who has grieved before and is now reaching out to help those newly mourning.

I began an online forum to reach out and find others to help at www.sistersinhope.com. At that site, widows who are well into their healing can offer help or a listening ear to those for whom the wounds are still fresh. Recent widows can ask questions, express their emotions in a safe place, and find a "sister" to walk through the grieving process with them.

Jillian Manus, a renowned literary agent, has created what she calls her "Broad Squad," a group of women friends with varying skills, talents, and expertise in different areas. They have all agreed to be there for each other whenever they can, and she knows she can call on them for help and that they'll be there. She has a doctor friend who she knows she can call in the middle of the night if her child has a fever to ask if it is serious enough to go to the emergency room. Another friend can counsel her about investments, and so on.

I, too, have an ever-expanding support group of women. We share everything from decorating ideas to recipes to emotional support and legal counsel. As you build your own sisterhood, do so prayerfully and carefully. Finding the right mix of personalities and knowledge takes time and intuition, but as you continually work at it and as you help each other through life's ups and downs, you'll find a sense of empowerment and strength.

There were many years when I felt I didn't have a friend with whom I could be really open. I thought the only person one should share their deepest feelings with was one's spouse. What, then, was one to do when the relationship with the spouse is strained, making sharing risky, or even impossible?

Once in one of the darkest times of my marriage, a dear friend perceived I was having difficulties and told me there may be times in a marriage when we aren't feeling love from our spouse and when the love of the Savior has to be sufficient. I rebelled at the thought; it didn't seem fair. I felt if one spouse was giving all they could, they could expect the other spouse to give in return.

She smiled, but her eyes held deep sadness. "No one can make another person give anything in a relationship. Sometimes our only friend, our only source of acceptance and love, is the Savior. And during those times, I attest His friendship is enough."

I couldn't see it. I wanted more. How could it be right to have to keep on giving, and yet not receive the validation I needed from my spouse? I went away from my friend disappointed and unhappy with her counsel.

It took me years to see that my friend was right, and that my reaction was immature. We can only give love. We cannot demand it in return.

C.S. Lewis, in his book *The Great Divorce,* shows two beings in Paradise reminiscing about life on Earth, and one says, "most of what we call love down there is a craving to be loved."

How true that can be in our lives. We give love, craving love in return. We expect an exchange, rather than the opportunity to simply love.

The friends who have come into my life since Marty's death have taught me about that kind of unconditional love and about giving simply for the sake of giving. They've lifted me and given me strength to keep moving even when I didn't think I could take one more step, and they did it with no thought of recompense or gain on their part.

John Donne's statement that "no man is an island" is certainly true while grieving. If we are to maintain perspective and hope as we move through the mourning process, we must find a friend.

ESSENTIAL TASKS FOR FINDING A FRIEND

- Pray in faith that you will find a friend to support you through this time. Believe that it will happen and then watch with an open mind and heart for God's direction.

- Visit and read the forum at www.sistersinhope.com. Create a profile and join in the conversation.

- Set up your sisterhood. Prayerfully select who you want to invite; set up some ground rules, and go for it!

- When you feel ready, become a friend to someone else. Reach out to someone you know who is grieving. Do one simple thing to lift their burden. Write a note, bake some cookies or simply make a point to greet them with a smile and a warm clasp of the hand.

- Check out local grief groups which are often listed on the community bulletin board of your local paper. Don't try to do all of your grieving alone. This is one path that is not always sweeter taken in solitude. There will be times when having a fellow traveler is the only thing that makes the journey bearable.

CHAPTER SEVEN

SET UP SYSTEMS

"Before everything else, getting ready is the secret of success."

— HENRY FORD —

The first time I heard the word systems used in association with our personal lives was years ago when I was sitting in a huge auditorium, and Dr. Oliver DeMille, the president of a private liberal arts college, had just asked the audience, "What systems do you have set up in your daily life?"

Systems? In my life? I'm just a mother! What on earth could he be talking about?

At that time, to me systems were something engineers employed in their designs. Factories used systems. Corporations used systems. Families? Absurd.

Yet Dr. DeMille proceeded to teach us that systems are essential to every success—even (and especially) the success of a family. I perceived that my interpretation of the word *system* was quite different from his.

As I sat listening, I came to understand his definition of systems: simply, a system is the way you have determined to accomplish something.

He stated that whether we have consciously developed them or not, we all have systems in our lives. For some people, the system for doing dishes is to wait until the sink and counter are full and the cupboards are bare – and then to hold a marathon dish-washing event. For others, the dishes are done completely after each meal. Each has a system; one is just much more effective than the other.

We've all heard of the routine familiar to our great-grandparents: Monday was washday, Tuesday ironing, Wednesday baking day, etc, etc. With all the modern conveniences we live with, that type of system is archaic and unnecessary now—isn't it? Haven't we been liberated from schedules like that?

Dr. DeMille continued his speech, saying that without effective systems, so many decisions are necessary each hour of the day that it becomes overwhelming, and discouragement can set in. However, he continued, with good systems in place, much of life runs on autopilot, and then one can focus on growth and progress much more easily.

Just think of all that goes into one day. Responding to the urgent needs of children, a home and a yard, coupled with work demands can eliminate any chance of achieving the essential tasks of the day. Decisions constantly have to be made regarding what is more important – this task or that one; this child's need or the desire to accomplish something on the never-ending list of things needing to be done.

At the end of such a day, it's hard to say just what has been accomplished—and the to-do list has hardly been shortened.

When you are grieving, you can be emotionally spent and distracted. Systems can help, especially in the initial period of grief, to take care of the daily basic necessities. Then, as you heal, systems will help you "cover all your bases" as a mother, grandmother, sister, daughter and homemaker; as a teacher, businesswoman, member of a religious congregation, etc.

Many women are blessed to have been "born organized", and systems seem innate to them. While grieving, they might only need to evaluate their situation and change one or two things to keep things running smoothly. However, the majority of the grieving women I have spoken to felt overwhelmed with all that needed to be done and agreed that systems would make a major improvement in their lives.

So where are systems needed, and how does one go about setting them up? That depends a great deal on one's lifestyle. A good starting point is to make a list of the things that absolutely have to happen each day, and see if you have a system in place to take care of each one. The very basics you will need to cover to keep the household running will include meals, laundry, finances, personal grooming, and basic cleanliness in the home.

If you have children, you need to apply all of the above to them also and care for their added emotional needs at this time. You'll need to arrange for them to get to wherever they need to go. School is a must; lessons, sports, and extracurricular activities can be put on hold for a time if you feel it is best for you and them. However, many families have found that the sooner life gets back to some semblance of normalcy, the better.

Depending on their ages, you could include the children in the decisions of what to do and what not to do right now. Simplify your schedule as much as possible until you can determine how much you can handle. Then decide where a system will help and implement it.

When I was floundering in the midst of my grief, I found a huge help in this area on a Web site a friend had recommended: www.flylady. com. "Flylady" (Marly Cilley) has developed a system for taking care of a home and family with what she calls "BabySteps." Starting with establishing the habit of keeping the kitchen sink "shiny clean", and then moving from there throughout the home, she helps a woman begin to create order in her home and her life. Through daily emails she reminds women to tackle the big chores fifteen minutes at a time, and soon, through following her suggestions, there are multiple systems in place keeping the home orderly.

Over the years I bought dozens of books on home organization. I read them all, but still struggled to maintain order in my home. The Flylady system is the first one I have been able to consistently maintain. Perhaps the key is her mantra, "You're not behind! Just jump in where you are!" Plenty of times I "fall off the wagon", get busy and miss completing my daily list of chores. But her constant loving, patient encouragement keeps me hopeful, drives off discouragement, and I just start over.

Where else can systems be helpful? In your religious life systems ensure regular prayer and study time, pondering, church attendance, and worship. Your health habits can be systematized, calendared and made a non-negotiable part of each day.

Menu-making and meal preparations are greatly simplified when put into a system. One system that radically changed our home I found in the book *Saving Dinner* by Leanne Ely. During the months when decisions still loomed like a huge barrier to my progress, this book made answering the question "What's for dinner tonight?" easy to answer. The book has menus divided into seasons, and for every weekly menu a complete shopping list is provided. I simply had to take the book to the grocery store (or print up the grocery list from Leanne's Web site), purchase the items on the list that I didn't have, and I was ready for the upcoming week.

Put in place a system for taking care of *you*. Now that you are alone, no one else is going to do it, and, as women, we often spend all our efforts taking care of everyone but ourselves. Don't let that happen. Decide how often you want a haircut, to do your nails, and take time out for relaxation, even if it is just to lock the bathroom door and take a long hot bath. Then create a system that will make sure it happens. Put it on the calendar; plan activities for the children,or exchange babysitting with another mom, and keep that "date" with yourself.

A system for finances is indispensable. Finances are such a vital, all-encompassing area of our lives that they merit their own chapter and will be addressed in Chapter Eight.

ESSENTIALS FOR SETTING UP SYSTEMS

- List the basics that have to be taken care of in your life right now. Be very choosy—there may be things you think need to be done that can actually be put off until you are more fully into your healing process.

- On the above list, put a checkmark by each task that you are confident is being taken care of in a timely manner and that doesn't cause you stress and doesn't need extra attention.

- Circle those that would benefit from having a system in place.

- Choose just one of the circled items to begin with—preferably the simplest one, and decide on a system that will help you streamline that task.

- Once you get one system in place, go back to your list and choose another to work on. If you "drop the ball" and let a system slide, refuse to get discouraged. Remember what Flylady says: You're not behind! Just jump in where you are!

CHAPTER EIGHT

FIX YOUR FINANCES

"Do you have any money?"

"Money? Oh no, we don't need that where I come from."

"Well it comes in pretty handy down here, bub."

— GEORGE BAILEY AND HIS GUARDIAN ANGEL

IN THE MOVIE *IT'S A WONDERFUL LIFE* —

"Have you made your house payment? Do you know how much money is in your bank account?"

The funeral was just two days away, and money was the last thing I wanted to be thinking about. I was confused why my friend was asking me about it.

"Roslyn, you need to go get the money out of your joint accounts so you'll have what you need to live on until you get things settled. I know it's awful to have to deal with this right now, but they could freeze your accounts when they receive word that Marty has died."

"Really? Why? It's my money, too." My mind was foggy and I was struggling to accept what she was telling me.

"If he has any debts you don't know about, or if there are issues with the bank, they'll want to be sure they are covered. Could you and your brother go down and take care of it first thing tomorrow? I could go with you if you'd like. It may be too late to take care of it if you wait until after the funeral."

I was about to learn how complicated the financial issues can be after losing one's spouse. Questions began flooding my mind. Did Marty have other bank accounts I wasn't aware of? When we had separated, I had opened my own account, and I knew he had one account in his own name because I had seen envelopes from a new credit union addressed to him in the mail. How could I get access to settle the account, if only his name was on the records?

My brother, Eldon, and I made a list of the accounts I knew of. The next day we took the house payment to the mortgage company, then drove to the credit union to transfer my money from our joint account into my personal account. I felt so uncomfortable, almost clandestine, like I was doing something wrong. I had to remind myself that he would want me to use this money to take care of the family. I was so relieved when it was over that as we walked out the door I heaved a huge sigh of relief.

As we climbed into the car Eldon said, "We need to make a list of all the financial things that need to be taken care of. Can you get some paper?" He pulled a pen and pad of paper from his pocket and made a duplicate list for himself as we talked. The list we came up with, and with which others dealing with loss will need to be familiar, includes the following:

1. **Life insurance:** Check on any life insurance—if possible, find the policy. Is it term or whole life; who are the beneficiaries, what is the expiration date, and was there accidental death coverage? What was the amount? Will it pay off the mortgage? (I couldn't find the policy for my husband. When I called the life insurance company,

they wouldn't tell me the amount of coverage. They told me I would have to wait until I received the check.)

2.   **Automobiles:** In whose name are they registered? If you have more than one car, will you keep all of them? Do you have loans on any of the cars? Can you pay them off and own the car free and clear? (My husband's car was in his name alone; the other two were in both names. I had to find out how to change the ownership and registrations.) You can wait for it to go through probate, or you can contact the county government and simplify the process.

3.   **Monthly bills:** Where do they all stand? Get them in order and make a monthly list detailing to whom each bill is to be paid, the date to be paid, the manner it is to be paid (automatic withdrawal, check, etc.) and the amount. Many women, especially if their late husband has been paying the bills, find using their financial institution's automatic bill-pay system is invaluable. Once set up, bills get paid on time each month without even a thought.

4.   **Bank accounts:** Find all bank accounts, both yours and your spouse's. List the name, account number, type of account (savings, checking, etc.), bank address and phone, signatories on the account, and dates opened. If your spouse received mail at his place of work, make sure you have it forwarded to you or arrange to pick it up. You need to establish a record of every financial correspondence your spouse might have had.

5.   **Credit cards:** How many are there? What are their balances? Do any of them have "credit life" coverage that pays off the balance upon the death of the primary card-holder? Record for each card where it is kept, the card number, expiration date, authorized co-signers, the balance, and the telephone number to report loss. Call on each card

your spouse had in his name and make an appointment if necessary to go in and close the account. Take all records that verify that you are the spouse. (I always took with me our will, our marriage certificate, Marty's death certificate, my driver's license and any bank records I had for that institution. Interestingly enough, I was never asked by a financial institution for the will. The only documents I was asked for were the bank statements, the death certificate, marriage certificate, and my driver's license. However that may not always be the case.)

6. **Insurance:** Homeowners, automobile, health—list each company, agency, policy number, name of insured, which cars or persons are insured, when they come due, and amount due.

7. **Investments**: Do you have any? With what brokerage firm? List the name, phone and address of the broker and location of certificate. If possible, list the initial investment, number of shares, price per share, commission, and total investment for each one.

8. **Safe deposit box**: Is there one? Record the box number, date opened, cost per year, names of those who have keys, authorized co-signers, and inventory.

9. **Probate:** This is when the court supervises the processes that transfer legal title of property from the estate of the person who has died (the decedent) to his or her beneficiaries. You may be able to avoid probate depending on the size of the estate and the circumstances at the time of death.

10. **Death certificate**: You will need one to present to each bank, medical provider, credit union, car title holder, investment company, insurance company, and financial institution. I ordered twenty and ended up using twelve. Even three years later, I occasionally find a need for one.

11. **Social Security**: Will you be eligible? Will the children? Ask around and find someone who knows the system to help you through this task.

12. **IRA or retirement accounts:** Where are they? List each one and what you need to do to change ownership to your name. For both traditional and Roth IRAs, this usually requires completion of a "designation of payment by beneficiary" form, after which time the account can be rolled over to the surviving spouse's name, or the funds can be withdrawn.

13. **Memberships**: Was he a member of any organizations that he might owe money to? Do you need to cancel any of his memberships? Also consider any memberships you may currently hold and determine which are wise to continue at this time.

14. **Estate plan**: If one is in place, list name of testator, location of original, location of copy, date executed, type of will or trust, personal representative, trustees, guardians, power of attorney, date of last codicil and who prepared it. If you don't have an estate plan, ask trusted friends or family for recommendations for a good attorney, and begin the process of setting one up. Even if your material assets are few and you don't consider them sufficient to call them an estate, having a plan in place will serve two purposes. You will have a clear picture of your financial standing (your net worth), and you and your family will be much better prepared for the future.

15. **Residential inventory:** Do you have one? If not, begin preparing one. Take photos of valuable items and list cost, date purchased, where acquired, location of sales receipt, and any appraisals done. Once complete, keep a copy for yourself, one with a trusted relative, and one online so you always have access to it. As you acquire new valuable items, be sure to include them in the inventory.

16. **Papers to gather**: Passports, birth certificates, auto titles, mortgage papers, marriage certificate, and Social Security cards. Keep them all in a fireproof safe. I bought a safe for under thirty dollars shortly after my husband died, but it is too small to hold all the documents I need in it. Consider what size will fit your needs before making this purchase.

17. **Gather names**: Attorney, accountant, stockbroker, physicians—list them all with phone numbers and contact information.

18. **Subscriptions:** Are there any subscriptions you need to be aware of? Did your spouse subscribe to professional or trade magazines? Are there any subscriptions you should cancel?

19. **Post office box:** Did your spouse have one for personal or business use? You will need to find the keys and arrange with the post office to either cancel it or transfer it into your name.

Your goal is to account for all of your resources and get them in the safest place. Alan Unger, author and financial counselor, said you can "turn money issues into the catalyst for accelerating your mending process." I like that thought. Instead of always looking at them as a stressful thing to have to deal with, as often as possible take the attitude that this will help you to heal. Getting on top of your finances will definitely make your life simpler, and you will be able to focus on other aspects of the healing process.

So look at each of the above categories, choose one to begin with, determine the first step to take, and then take it.

Notice the first six steps mentioned in the cycle of grief: shock, numbness, denial, confusion, anger, guilt, depression, and loneliness. Are any of those conducive to being decisive or responsible? While we are in the midst of those steps and living life largely through our emotions, we need a way to, for at least a few minutes each day, fix our finances. If we simply start by going online daily to see what our balance is, it is much better than ignoring our finances and risking falling further and further behind.

I highly recommend finding an experienced financial counselor that you feel comfortable with, who understands your priorities, and who has your financial well-being as his first concern. I met with several before I found the one I felt I could communicate with easily and that I wanted to work with. Find someone you can trust who has been wise with their money and go over all your options with them. You may find that having someone with whom to discuss any major financial decisions is invaluable. They can give you their perspective and guidance, and you will be able to make more informed decisions after counseling with them.

Here are some general caveats to consider.

Be cautious about making any major financial decisions at first. Don't immediately take the insurance money and remodel the house or purchase a new car. Keep any insurance settlement money in a safe but accessible place until you've had sufficient time to choose your options wisely. A money market or a short-term CD could be a good option. Only invest in long-term investments once you feel ready to make that decision wisely and are certain you have the necessary amount of funds for short-term needs in easily accessible accounts. Financial guru Dave Ramsey suggests never investing in anything until you understand it well enough to explain it to a sixth-grader. I think that's good advice.

Be wary of taking advice only from family members or close friends without running it past a neutral third party. I've heard some sad stories of women who invested on the advice of a family member or friend which later brought disastrous results.

You may end up with a large lump sum of insurance. It is not unheard of for a family member or close friend to ask for a loan. Richard Paul Evans suggests making it a rule whenever asked for money to tell the person, "My financial consultant has asked me to run all requests past him. I'll talk to him and get back to you." Especially when someone asks for money to start a business, promising to pay the loan back out of the profits of the business, it is vital to protect yourself by asking them for their business plan, and then tell them you will have your advisor look it over and let you know what they suggest. Take their proposal to your trusted advisor and consultant. When appropriate, he can then be the "bad guy" and relieve some of the pressure from you having to say no to a financial move that could prove ruinous.

Do make sure you have medical and disability insurance. I know that monthly amount takes a huge chunk out of your income, but if a medical emergency happened, without insurance you could end up hundreds of thousands of dollars in debt. That is the last thing you need when you are recovering from tragic loss.

Face it. It can very difficult to face our financial situation. The "head in the sand" reaction can feel much safer, less threatening, and simpler. Richard Paul Evans speaks about the woman he met who showed him her "Magic Bill Drawer": whenever she received a bill, she would stick it in the drawer, and it "disappeared", never to be seen again. But not facing our situation can have disastrous repercussions as I experienced.

One Saturday morning in May, I was in a bookstore at the cash register when the clerk said to me, "I'm sorry, ma'am. Your card was declined."

He had dropped his voice and leaned slightly closer to me to say it. I felt my cheeks grow hot and red, and I stammered,

"I—I don't know what's wrong. It should be fine, "

I shifted my weight to the other foot. In my mind I was going over all the expenditures of the last several days. Could I really have gone through nine hundred dollars in that period of time? The clerk continued looking at me, and I scrambled for a way to redeem the situation. I needed to buy the books—what would I take to my mother and mother-in-law for Mothers' Day tomorrow if not these? I thought about my money market account—I could withdraw cash from there to pay for them.

"I'll run across the street to the credit union and get cash. Can you hold them, and I'll be right back?"

"Sure thing. I'll hold them back here," he said as he placed the bag behind the counter and began to help the next customer.

I turned toward the door without looking back to see who had been behind me in line. I didn't want to risk seeing someone I knew and being even more embarrassed by what had just transpired.

As I hurried over to the credit union ATM across the street, I felt hopeless. Just last month I had walked out to the curb to check the mailbox and, going back toward the house, I was leafing through the mail when the sight of one envelope made my heart drop. I swallowed hard, glanced up at the windows of the house and slipped the envelope into the pile of grocery ads. I felt ashamed, as if everyone in the neighborhood would know what I was hiding in that pile of mail.

I hurried through the front door, closed it, and leaned back against it. How could this have happened? I had thought for sure I would have plenty of money this month with the last check I had received. Yet here in my hands was that familiar envelope from the credit union that I was sure every mailman recognized: non-descript, plain white with my name and address showing through the clear window, bearing yet another overdraft notice.

It hurt too much to blame myself. I couldn't stand the thought that it was all my fault. So I justified myself. It couldn't be my fault. How could I be expected to handle all the emotions I was experiencing, deal with the children and all their needs, stay on top of all the household tasks *and* take care of the finances too? Nobody could do all that. Or so I told myself. It was much more comfortable to slip into victim mode where I didn't have to accept the responsibility for any problems. I had suffered so much. I did have a hard life right now. There were people who reminded me of that over and over. Who could expect me to handle everything? I laid the newspapers on the counter, took the letter opener out of the drawer and slit open the envelope. Two checks had bounced—one of them was written for only $2.95, yet now it had cost me $19 in insufficient funds fees to buy that now-forgotten three dollar item.

The longer I thought about it, the more disgusted with myself I became. Who else could be accountable for this? No one else had access to my accounts, and there was only one place to lay the blame.

I sat at the table and opened my checkbook. Every check was written down, but no balance was carried forward. I always felt rushed at the store when filling out the check, and I just knew the people behind me in line would be impatient if I took the time to bring the balance down while they waited. So I would quickly write the check, or swipe the debit card, and assume the money would be there to cover it.

I thought back over my financial life. From the time I was in college and I'd repeatedly had to call my father to tell him I had run out of money again, and then all through the years of my marriage, money had been a difficult topic—and therefore had been avoided until absolutely necessary. That had usually been too late to remedy the situation without major inconvenience and embarrassment.

Neither of us had been very good with money. I remember a string of Christmases when my husband and I would buy each other gifts we didn't know if we could afford, and then make our annual day-after-Christmas trip to return them.

Now here I was on my own, and I had to face the problem. It *was* my responsibility. And if I didn't fix it now, it would continue to haunt me the rest of my life—and most likely cause problems for my children too.

Thousands of authors have addressed the topic of establishing wise financial habits. I have several shelves filled with financial books in my study. I'd read most of them, yet still I needed help. Was there one that would change me, make me the responsible adult I hoped I appeared to be, but that I knew I was not?

I went to the study and pulled out one pamphlet and the smallest book. The three-page pamphlet, published by my church, is entitled *All Is Safely Gathered In: Family Finances*. And the book was *The Five Lessons A Millionaire Taught Me About Life and Wealth* by Richard Paul Evans. I felt by using these two guides, I could plan a new beginning.

The pamphlet suggests five keys to finding security and peace in our financial efforts. The keys are:

Pay tithes and offerings

Avoid debt

Use a budget

Build a reserve

Teach family members

Those seemed to be simple enough guidelines that I could discipline myself to follow each one. I decided to begin right away.

I picked up the *Five Lessons* book. Scanning down through the chapter headings I remembered the five things the author wrote about that could change one's financial situation. I felt I could do five things. And I liked the word "millionaire". Was there hope of me ever getting there? Probably not, starting at this point in my life—but I could certainly do better than I was presently doing. I had to start somewhere, and it had to be now. I decided these were the two programs I would follow for now.

The five lessons are: Decide to be wealthy, take responsibility for your money, keep a portion of everything you earn, win in the margins, and give back.

Decide to be wealthy. Mr. Evans suggests that one of the biggest hurdles we may have to jump is our negative emotional reaction when we think of being "wealthy". For many of us, the often incompletely-quoted Bible verse, "money is the root of all evil," colors our perception of having money. The complete verse reads, "The *love* of money is the root of all evil," which changes the meaning considerably. But if that is a problem for us, Evans asks us to consider that money is what provides the necessities of life and allows us to take care of our families. Money is what allows us to help others and to create beauty. He asks, "What would the world be like if only the evil people had money? Would there be churches, or parks, or libraries and museums?" Overcoming that emotional bias is the first step to take on our road to creating wealth.

Take responsibility for your money. This means knowing our net worth, and then setting up a system to track how much money we have, where it comes from, where it is going, and what it is doing. Is it earning money for us? Could it do better if we invested it differently?

Just as we all think a little differently from each other, we have ways of doing things that "fit" or make sense to us. The system that works for me may be comfortable to you. However it is absolutely vital to find and stick with *some* system and use it regularly. This allows you to always know where you stand financially.

When I went to Google and entered "income and spending tracking systems," it brought up 316,000 responses. There are plenty of choices out there. I have tried some pretty sophisticated systems over the years, but I found that the simpler the better. I settled on "The Money Planner" by Chequemate International because of its simplicity and ease of use. Whatever system you settle on, make sure it is one you can understand and that makes it easy to see how you are progressing.

Keep a portion of everything you earn. Mr. Evans teaches that if you don't develop the habit of saving, you will never achieve true wealth, no matter how much money you bring in each month.

Win in the margins. Find ways to add to your growing nest egg through extra income and savings. There are many ways we can become more productive and make our time and effort count more than once. Starting a home-based business is just one way.

Give back. I long to be able to make a big difference in the lives of large numbers of people. Richard Paul Evans teaches that we need to start right now, because "the most honorable and enjoyable use of money is in serving others." He proposes that giving will also help us build wealth and says, "While generosity feeds the soul, ironically it also feeds the pocketbook. I believe that we receive as we give." I have found great joy in giving just a small amount each month, knowing that it is blessing lives, and I look forward to the day when, by building greater wealth in my own life, I will have greater abundance to share with those in need.

As in all other aspects of healing from loss, when we deal with finances, I have found again that it is helpful to have support from others. They can be there when we are unsure of making a purchase to encourage us to keep working toward a financial goal, or to keep us accountable as we agree to report back on a regular basis regarding how we are doing financially.

There are several books I have found that have different views on finances, or that expand on different principles, and I frequently leaf through one or another of them to find what I need at the moment. This helps me continue learning, take responsibility for my money, and understand the best ways to deal with the whole subject. By keeping these books in plain sight, and referring to them occasionally, I am able to keep myself motivated to work toward my financial goals.

Some of the most helpful books I have found are:

- *The Five Lessons A Millionaire Taught Me About Life and Wealth for Women* by Richard Paul Evans

- *The One Minute Millionaire* by Mark Victor Hansen and Robert G. Allen

- *Personal Finance for Dummies* by Eric Tyson

- *Financial Peace* by Dave Ramsey

- *Debt Proof Living* by Mary Hunt

- *The Complete Cheapskate* by Mary Hunt

- *The Four Laws of Debt Free Prosperity* by Blaine Harris and Charles Coonradt

- *Financial Self-Confidence for the Suddenly Single* by Alan. B. Unger *(out of print but available at libraries and can be purchased used online)*

- *Survivor Support Reference Guide 2006* from The Ayco Company, L.P.

SMART STEPS TO TAKE NOW
FOR YOUR FINANCIAL FUTURE

- Designate one place for all your financial information to be kept. Purchase file folders and choose a file box, filing cabinet, or drawer that will hold them and begin creating your financial document depository. Download or copy the *Fix Your Finances* forms from the appendix and start gathering your documents and getting everything in one place. Begin filling out information as you come across the appropriate documents.

- Set up a support system. Arrange with someone—a trusted friend, sister, brother, etc.—to check in with you at regular intervals and get updates on how you are doing financially. Knowing you have to report back can make getting the unpleasant tasks done a higher priority and reduces the risk of you putting them off continually.

- Make every arrangement you can that insures you are cared for. If you have balances on credit cards, arrange for "credit life" coverage to make sure they are paid off in the event of your death or disability. Make sure all vital life and health insurance is in place.

CHAPTER NINE

DITCH THE D's

I stood in the kitchen gazing out the window at the apricot tree, heavy with fruit, its branches swaying in the light breeze. I took another bite of the warm peanut-butter cookie just out of the oven and enjoyed the creamy texture as it coated my mouth. I lifted the chilled glass of milk to my lips, and felt the tiny ice crystals swirling around my tongue as the two flavors joined. Warm chewy cookies and ice-cold milk . . . mmmm, a combination hard to pass up.

Especially hard, lately. Why was I standing here eating cookies when just two days ago I had been so upset at myself when the zipper on my skirt had been so hard to pull up and I had made a commitment to try harder this week to eat wisely? What was I thinking? That this cookie wouldn't make a difference? That for some reason just this time it would be all right to indulge, and next Sunday, when I try to put on that skirt, somehow that zipper will slide right up without effort?

I hate to admit it, but I like to live in denial. It is much more comfortable to ignore the consequences of my choices, and I much prefer doing just what I want to, rational or not, and not thinking about where that action might lead.

However, I realize that most of the time I deny that I live in denial. It's been my experience that denial is most easily spotted in someone else. Like pride, it is rarely, if ever, a self-diagnosed problem. I can plainly see when someone else is responding with denial in their life, but for some reason it is almost impossible for me to discern my deceitful whispers to myself. *"It won't be a problem, just this once." "You deserve this. You've had it hard." "You'll love how this tastes. It will make you feel better." "You look great the way you are."*

A dear friend wrote me about her mother, a widow living alone. "Mom won't consider leaving her home. She has severe short-term memory loss and forgets everything. Reads the same books over and over because she can't remember new ones. Can't cook because she can't remember what she put in and what she didn't. She won't consider living with her children although we all want her. We are concerned for her safety. She has left the house with doors standing open, forgotten where she is driving, where she has parked the car. We want her to set up a living will, but she will not even consider it. She is alone and lonely, but won't do anything to change that."

Denial has a way of affecting each of us. I live in an area of homes built on the side of a mountain. In the mornings when I go walking I can either walk parallel to the valley floor along the wide streets and boulevards and not encounter too many hills, or when I feel a need for a real workout, I can head straight uphill.

The hill is not at a perfect ascending angle. There are dips and rises as it climbs the mountainside. There is one section of the road where the dip is deep enough that, to my perspective as I walk uphill, a car coming down the hill disappears. It is an optical illusion because at that point it looks like there is no dip—as if the road is connected from the point I can see at the bottom to the point that is visible above the dip. It looks like one continuous ribbon of road.

On warm summer mornings, to take advantage of the shade and to receive the refreshing cooling mist from the occasional sprinkler, I often cross the road at this point. I have learned that I need to be watching the road above the dip as I climb the hill so that I know if I will have time to cross safely. If I do not keep my eyes on the hill above, I may be caught unaware and end up right in the pathway of a fast-approaching car.

Sometimes I become involved in whatever I am listening to that morning and forget to look up. I get to that point, glance up and, seeing nothing, I start to cross. Yet not infrequently my ears catch that low warning hum, and I look up to see the roof of a car appearing above the dip—and I have to run for my life.

How often do we do things like that in life? We know there are potential problems with what we are doing, yet we choose not to think about or deal with them, hoping they'll disappear in the dip, and never reappear. What can we do if we find ourselves sabotaging our progress through denial? How can we spot it in our life?

One technique is to step back for a few moments each week to evaluate our life. Where are we ineffective in what we want to be accomplishing? Is it our weight, a relationship? Could it be our spirituality or our homemaking? Identifying where we might be indulging in denial is the first step.

Next we must look and see what laws we are breaking and where our choices are out of line with reality. There are natural laws that govern pretty much everything we do. If we break the law, progress is hampered or even halted. If we are choosing to act in a way that defies reason, we need to recognize that fact, admit it and be willing to find ways to change our behavior.

For example, I want to lose weight. I love the feeling of a zipper sliding up without effort. When I eat with abandon, the weight begins to pile on, and the zipper refuses to budge. At that point, I know it is time to lose some weight.

However, the laws for weight loss require fewer calories coming into the system or a change in eating habits, and more calories being expended through increased movement and exercise. If I don't follow those laws, I won't get the results I want.

Why do we sometimes refuse to acknowledge things that are making life difficult and frustrating for us and others, and even unsafe? Why do we resist confronting those things that are holding us back from the success we would see if we'd only address them?

John Baker, in *Life's Healing Choices*, says it is our human nature to deny our need to change. Change is difficult. We want to feel like we are okay just as we are. If we finally admit—which is rare—that there is a problem, we think we can fix the problem on our own power. He says, "we try to fix problems, and often in our attempts to fix them, we only make them worse." His cure? Admit our weakness, cultivate a humble heart, and turn to God.

I have found the same thing. When I finally admit that I need to work on a challenge that I haven't been able to overcome on my own, I only begin to see progress when I humbly ask God for His help.

The Four D's

After the death of my husband, I found that the grieving process held several pitfalls that could derail my progress. I call them the Four D's. In my effort now to help others learn how to heal after a tragic loss, I find that if the Four D's are watched for and dealt with, recovery is greatly accelerated. If ignored, progress is impeded. I have realized that in order to heal from a loss, and we all have losses of one sort or another, we need to ditch the D's.

Denial is one D. What are the other three? Discouragement, depression and despair. Each differs from the others in degree and effects.

Discouragement is literally being deprived of courage or confidence. The trials of everyday life are enough to dishearten most people at one time or another. When the loss of a loved one occurs, life can look especially fearsome, and discouragement is common.

Depression defined is "a pressing down, or lowering; a state of feeling sad; a psychological disorder marked especially by sadness, inactivity, difficulty in thinking and concentration, and feelings of dejection."

My sister-in-law, Pat, defines it as "depressing your true feelings instead of letting them out, or stuffing your feelings." When we stuff our feelings, they have nowhere to go but inward, affecting our attitude and our peace of mind. If severe, depression can make life seem too difficult to face and lead to withdrawal and feelings of hopelessness. Some columnists have called depression the epidemic of our age. It is widespread and statistics show it is growing.

Despair is defined as "the utter loss of all hope or confidence." Once a person has lost all hope, life has no value to them, and despair can even lead to suicide.

When the task of moving on after loss is considered, with all that needs to be done, denial, discouragement, depression and despair can easily set in. However, there are ways to lessen and even overcome these great challenges if we learn them and put them to use. I have compiled a list of those things that I have found most helpful in defusing the D's, and they are as follows: music, health, work, repentance, fasting, reading, writing, goals, wise counsel, and endurance.

Music

There is a very real pain associated with deep sorrow and despair. Beautiful soul-stirring music can ease that pain and lift one's heart out of despair and bring hope. It can infuse sunshine into a soul darkened by depression and create an opening in the clouds of discouragement that block the sun.

I realize that when I speak about music, that word means different things to different people. Some music lifts the spirit, while other music has been proven to *bring on* depression and even lead to suicide. Some music tends to remove inhibitions and lower standards, while other music inspires courage, heightens sensitivity, and encourages refinement.

Socrates noted that some harmonies increase sorrow, some encourage indolence, some inspire courage, and others encourage temperance. Aristotle suggested that in listening to music our souls undergo a change, and the type of music we are listening to determines the type of change we experience.

Music has played a major part in my healing. There were times when my heart was so heavy and the ache so profound that I felt I could not bear it. One thing that I found helpful was listening to beautiful music turned up so loud I felt I was in the concert hall. The Mormon Tabernacle Choir CDs were the most powerful influence in helping me to bear my sorrow because not only was the music moving, but the lyrics reminded me of God's love for me and His promise to always be near, in joy or sorrow.

Michael Ballam, the renowned opera singer, has shared research documenting that great music can calm the heart rate, soothe the nerves and emotions, and replace agitation with peacefulness. The music I recommend to help overcome discouragement, depression and despair is the music that has been shown to have these effects on the soul.

The research Mr. Ballam quotes cites the music of Handel, Mozart, Beethoven and other composers from the classical period as especially effective in quieting anxiety and promoting feelings of hope, peace and calm. If we are not familiar with this style of music, it might be wise to learn about it in order to appreciate it and use it to lift our spirits.

Douglas L. Callister, speaking to students at Brigham Young University said, "When some music has passed the tests of time and been cherished by the noble and refined, our failure to appreciate it is not an indictment of grand music. The omission is within. If a young person grows up on a steady diet of hamburgers and French fries, he is not likely to become a gourmet. But the fault is not with fine food. He just grew up on something less. Some have grown up on a steady diet of musical French fries."[5]

Making an effort to learn to appreciate that "grand music" and then using it in our daily lives can make a significant difference in our ability to ditch the D's. See a list of suggested musical selections in the Appendix.

HEALTH

We all know that if our health is poor, nothing else in life goes as smoothly. If we ignore our health, disease and illness are more likely to occur, and then our health can soon become our main focus. If, on the other hand, we make taking care of our health a priority, eating wisely and getting regular exercise and sufficient rest, not only are we getting those endorphins flowing, but we are strengthening our body against disease and injury. When we are in good health, our frame of mind can be more positive, and we can focus our energies on becoming emotionally whole.

I recently attended a seminar addressing good health habits, and the presenter taught that dehydration often causes many of the same symptoms as depression. Drinking enough clean water is a vitally important but often overlooked component of a healthy daily routine, and one that is relatively easy to incorporate.

No one else can do this for us—we each need to make the commitment to take care of our health.

WORK

When dealing with discouragement, depression and despair, often the last thing we want to do is tackle a big project. However, work is often the very best antidote to low spirits.

---

5 Douglas L. Callister, "Your Refined Heavenly Home," BYU devotional address, 6 November 1994.

Mindy's husband was flying home with his friend in a small airplane when the plane crashed, killing them both instantly. Mindy was provided with sufficient life insurance that if she never did anything to bring in money, she'd be taken care of. However, she feels that pursuing meaningful work is what keeps her attitude positive and her thoughts turned outward toward others. "I volunteer four hours a week," she wrote. "My time spent helping others cheers my heart and fills my need for companionship as we talk and process together." She is constantly involved with projects and causes that make a difference for those she is serving, and in the process, her life is brightened, too.

In some of the beginning verses in the Bible we read that when God cursed the ground he told Adam that the cursing was "for thy sake". In other words, the hard work of eating bread "by the sweat of thy face" was meant to be a blessing.

In our society, where ease and recreation are prized so highly, why should we believe that work can help us when we are feeling down? Don't we need a break instead?

I don't believe so for at least two reasons.

First, one of man's basic needs is to be needed, to feel worthwhile, and to have something to show for being alive. Finding some work that needs to be done, that one can do well, and then doing it, creates a sense of accomplishment, boosting one's self-confidence and self-esteem.

Second, getting out and moving the muscles causes endorphins to flow. Endorphins are neurotransmitters that are sometimes called the "happy hormones" because they create a feeling of euphoria and reduce the effects of pain and stress. Everyone can use more endorphins flowing through their system.

If we want to ditch depression, discouragement and despair, we need to get to work.

REPENTANCE

Repentance simply means change. We recognize where we have been wrong, admit it, make the commitment to change, and move forward. To be at peace, we must act in line with our core values. When we have acted or spoken in a manner that violates those values, our soul feels the chasm, the subconscious mind is unsettled, and depression can set in.

When we do wrong and we know it, but we want to justify our actions, we create an inner dichotomy. The authors at the Arbinger Foundation say that in this we are practicing "self-deception". When we deceive ourselves, we become less "real", and because our soul craves integrity and genuineness, we are less at peace. People have come up with all sorts of ways to deal with the feeling of being out-of line with their core, from filling their time so fully that they can't think about it, to turning to drugs and other ways to artificially raise—or dull—their spirits. However, when being out of line with our core beliefs is the diagnosis, the quickest most effective way to find peace is to repent. To feel at peace, we need to have a clear conscience.

Ogden Nash said, "There is only one way to achieve happiness on this terrestrial ball, and that is to have either a clear conscience or none at all."

As we repent, make changes, and find our conscience cleared, we can find greater happiness.

FASTING

Fasting is going without food or drink for a specified amount of time. Health professionals have long agreed that occasional brief fasting, usually for a period of twenty-four hours, clears the system and has multiple benefits physically. However, fasting also allows us to focus more intently on our spiritual, intuitive needs. As we fast, we are more in tune spiritually and can draw nearer to our Maker, evaluate our life more intently, and receive insight as to how we can best move ahead and improve our life. (As with all dietary considerations, consult with your medical doctor before beginning a fast.)

READING

Reading can be a way to overcome the D's, depending on what you are reading. I have started some books that, rather than leading away from depression, would ensure a person ends up there. I close those books and move on. I saw a sign once that read, "When you find a book is poor, spend no more time upon it." That is good counsel. Great literature can entertain us, lift us, instill important lessons, and teach us to think.

In our busy lives, how do we make time to read?

Louis L'Amour said in his autobiography, "Often I hear people say they do not have time to read. That's absolute nonsense. In the one year during which I kept that kind of record, I read twenty-five books while waiting for people. In offices, . . . waiting to see a dentist, waiting in a restaurant for friends . . . I read on buses, trains, and planes. If one really wants to learn, one has to decide what is important. Spending an evening on the town? Attending a ball game? Or learning something that can be with you your life long?"

First on the list of literature I find helpful is scripture. The Bible used to be considered the "core" book of the United States because it was one book that most people read and were familiar with. There is good reason for that. Not only did it provide common stories and philosophies for people to refer to and to build society around, but the faith in God that it taught was a source of hope and stability in times of tragedy and trial. It can be so today. Reading the word of God is one main way to become closer to God, to understand how He deals with His people, and how He wants us to conduct our lives. As we read from the scriptures, we can feel God's influence in our lives and gain strength from the truths therein. Reading the stories in the scriptures can be a very real calming influence and is able to lift the soul in a way very few other things can. We can see how people before us dealt with tragedy and challenges, and gain insight that will help us deal with our own trials.

Douglas L. Callister spoke of overhearing a church leader lament the fact that he never had time for anything except to read the scriptures and other works of literature and to prepare talks. The leader's wife admiringly responded, "I know, dear. We all know. We know every time you stand up to speak." As he spoke, listeners saw. The unremitting preparation through a lifetime of reading great literature naturally produced eloquent messages."[6]

Ruth, while suffering from depression, said, "I put myself on a diet of humor. I subscribed to Reader's Digest and found other sources of clean humor and made it a point to read something funny every day— and to share it with someone too. Both things helped."

Over the years I have compiled a list of books I can turn to that I know will draw me in, lift my spirits, make me laugh, or fill my soul with warmth. You can make a similar list and keep those books handy for the dark days.

Our reading can be an escape, a source of enjoyment, and a way to relax and overcome discouragement. In addition, if we choose wisely what we read, study out of the greatest books, and include the scriptures in our daily reading, our reading can also become preparation for whatever the future holds for us.

To find greater happiness, make time to read great books.

---

6 Douglas L. Callister, "Your Refined Heavenly Home," BYU devotional address, 6 November 1994.

WRITING

IPods, MP3 players, video games, Wii, iPhones, cell phones, Kindles, TV, movies, radio—the list is endless. There are abundant places for us to find something to do, to listen to, or to watch to lift our spirits. But we sometimes forget how powerful two items dating from the first century AD and 1795 AD, respectively, can be—paper and pencil. Writing can be a potent force for good as we strive to push through the dark clouds of despair.

Some counselors suggest writing daily journal entries describing what you are feeling, and why you feel that way—if you can discern that—and ending each entry with one thing for which you can be grateful. Just writing that one positive item can mark the beginning of your ascent into the light.

Some days that last item may be hard to come up with. "The house is still standing." "Little Trevor's ears are still in the right place." Something, *anything* that focuses on a positive note, can help you realize that yes, you're in a hard place, but there is always *something* positive in your life. And if there is *one,* there are bound to be two or more. Keep looking and keep writing.

This writing exercise serves to open up a portion of the brain that seems to close down when we approach depression—the creative, "artist brain," as author Julia Cameron calls it. In her book, *The Artist's Way,* she suggests writing every morning upon arising. Calling them "morning pages", she suggests writing three pages of longhand writing, strictly stream-of-consciousness, at the beginning of each day to clear the clutter from the brain and allow it to be open to inspiration and creativity. I have to admit I rarely get in three full pages, but the days I begin the day by writing, I do have a clearer mind and everything seems to go better.

There is so much constant "noise" going on in our brains. Much of what is there has not been put there by our own conscious choice, but flows in from our surroundings. Jacques Lusseyran calls it "the pollution of the I." We need to constantly take note of what is passing through our mind, remove that which is hampering our efforts at recovery, and replace it with truth and peace.

I have found that as I write out the thoughts, questions and impressions that are in my mind, just letting them all flow out onto the paper, I get to a point where there is no longer the confusion and noise, but order and peace—and quiet. When I get to that point, I achieve a clarity I can reach in no other way, opening my mind to inspiration and creativity and hopefulness.

WISE COUNSEL

I emerged from childhood with the perception that only "crazy" people went to counseling. The title, "Psychiatrist," brought images to my mind of an old Jerry Lewis movie with the client lying on a couch, and the prying doctor in a white coat, clipboard and pen in hand, coaxing deep, dark secrets out of the hypnotized patient.

Many people share the conception that counseling is at best unnecessary, and at worst dangerous. However, I have come to believe that there are some situations and times where a neutral third party, prayerfully and carefully chosen, well trained in human nature, can help us see things from a clearer perspective and with new eyes.

There are times when we get stuck in negative patterns of thought and behavior, and we can't see why things aren't improving. A wise counselor can help us to recognize negative patterns and suggest new, healthier ways to respond and act. Following their counsel can help us loosen chains that have bound us for years and make us free to move on, changing and improving our lives.

Goals

Part of the problem with discouragement, depression and despair is that we are focused on the difficulties of the past and the trial we are currently going through. We fail to look ahead, except with fear.

Setting a goal gives us something to aim and hope for—something good in the future to anticipate. Plus it reinforces the thought that we *do* have power to change our lives, one step at a time.

A goal doesn't need to be huge to be life changing. I remember feeling very discouraged shortly after the birth of my fifth child. I was standing at the sink washing dishes, looking out the window at the bare trees on a cold, rainy late-autumn day. Depression was creeping in, and I felt the dark cloud begin to envelope my soul.

As tears began to cloud my vision, I prayed.

"Father, help me. I need help to go on. I don't feel I can do this anymore."

Immediately, warmth washed over me, from head to toe, and a thought entered my mind.

"Smile more."

That was it. Two words. But those two words were life changing. From that moment on, I decided to accept the challenge, and I made it a goal to smile whenever I felt discouragement creeping back in.

That small change made a difference in my life, and I know it made a difference in the lives of my children. I had become unhappy and impatient in my discouragement, and it had affected our home. I didn't always feel like smiling when I needed to, but I remembered my goal and that whisper from God, and I smiled. Somehow the curve of my lips changed the tone in my heart and in our home. The answer to my prayer was no doubt the answer to the prayers of five small children too.

ENDURANCE

In our culture of instant fixes, we want solutions to our problems and we want them *now*. But when dealing with the D's, there may be times when nothing removes the problem, and we just have to "stick it out." Widows know that feeling, and others dealing with long-term deep disappointment know it also.

My sister, Ruth, has dealt for most of her life with the repercussions of a genetic disorder requiring more than thirty-three surgeries over the years. She has dealt with extended hospital stays, months of wearing casts, inconvenience, discomfort, and pain. In spite of the physical challenges she has faced, she has determined to remain positive, even hopeful, through it all.

Ruth has collected humorous sayings to post on the walls in her hospital room whenever another surgery is necessary, and doctors, nurses, and others visit her room frequently to see what she has on her wall that day. "Cheer up! Even Moses was once a basket case!" "Even if you have pains, you don't have to be one!" "An apple a day keeps the doctor away—if you throw hard and your aim is accurate." (See Appendix for more.) The quotes not only lift her spirits, but those of everyone around her.

Living with long-term difficulty is a challenge, but there are ways to help lift the burden so it is more bearable. For example, when Ruth was diagnosed with an ulcer, she gave the ulcer a name—Henrietta. She found that giving the disorder a name changed her perspective from "Poor me because I have an ulcer" to "I will not be defined by this ulcer!" When decisions about what she could or could not eat became necessary, she would say to herself, "I won't eat that because I don't want Henrietta to be upset with me." It allowed her to see *herself* as empowered, dealing wisely with the challenge of a new condition. It also lightened the mood and shed the light of humor onto what could have been seen as another heavy burden.

Ruth understands endurance. Like Paul in 2 Corinthians, we may have a "thorn in the flesh" that will not be removed during this life that we simply need to learn to live with. But as we determine to make the best of each situation and just to hold on and keep going, we will find the strength to live *and* to find happiness in spite of our problems.

EMERGENCY KIT

Several years ago I attended with a loved one some counseling sessions for overcoming addiction. One suggestion they gave to those struggling with addiction was to put together an "emergency kit"—something portable to have in their car or wherever they went, with items in it that would help them to pull out of the downward spiral and remind them of their commitments. I suggest we can do the same for those times when any of the D's threaten to descend.

Make your own kit. Some items I like to have close are an upbeat CD, a picture of my children, a drawing from my grandson, some of my favorite scripture verses, some poems that make me smile, a few affirmations, and a snack that I can reward myself with when I succeed in warding off the "attack." You can use anything that will turn your thoughts away from darkness and toward the light.

Our trials can either send us into denial, discouragement, depression, and despair or we can come to use them as an opportunity to make changes, to grow, and to see how our Maker is working in our life.

Sometimes we feel so miniscule, and these D's can seem like giants standing in our way, blocking our progress. I am reminded of the coach of a small-town football team, portrayed in the movie *Facing the Giants*. Against all odds, the understaffed team made it to the State football playoffs, and they were fearful of facing the long-standing State Champions, the Giants.

As the coach was leaving the locker room to enter the field before the big game, a friend of his, a coach of a professional team, approached him and asked him how he was doing. The coach admitted his fear, and his friend reminded him, "In God's word he says 365 times, 'Do not fear!' If he said it that many times, he must mean it."

The coach of the small-town team then went out to give his players one last word of encouragement. "Men," he said, "as long as we honor God, nothing is impossible."

To that team, the best way to overcome their fear was to go out, do their best, fight their hardest, and trust that God would take care of the rest.

On our dark days we must remember that. I keep two scriptures posted where I can see them frequently. From 1 Timothy 4: "I can do all things through Christ, which strengtheneth me" and from Colossians Chapter 3: ". . . whatsoever ye do, do it heartily, as to the Lord, and not unto men . . ." As I go about my daily tasks, it helps me to think that I am doing them for Him. When I do things well, it honors God. As I try to do my best—which some days is simply making it through another day—He makes up the rest, and I feel peace.

That is our covenant—we honor God with every moment of our lives and allow Him to do whatever He will with them. As we put our heart into that work and begin to see His hand supporting us, our eyes will be opened to the things we are denying, and our hearts will begin to fill with light, driving out the darkness of discouragement, depression, and despair.

ESSENTIAL TASKS FOR DITCHING THE D's

- Pray for strength and for God's grace to help you recognize when one of the D's is affecting you. Recognizing is the first step to overcoming.

- Start your list of things that make your "happy hormones" flow. Is it listening to the Bee Gees? Or Rachmaninoff? Is it hiking? Painting? Reading Dickens? Begin your list in a place you can continually add to. It will grow over the weeks and months and become the first place you turn when you need a lift.

- Consciously determine to be your own D's patrol. The moment you feel one of the D's approaching, or notice a downward-leading thought, reject it. Don't let yourself dwell on the negative. Put on some music, call a friend, or go to www.sistersinhope.com for support and ideas.

- Build your emergency kit and carry it with you. Use it.

- Take care of your health. Drink and eat what truly nourishes your body and get out and move in some way daily. Endorphins are some of our greatest allies in this fight against the D's.

- Start a "gratitude journal"—a place to record every day at least one thing you are grateful for.

CHAPTER TEN

BUILD BELIEF IN YOURSELF

"I can't do *anything*. All I have ever done is be a wife and mother. I'm totally *useless*," Carol whispered as she stared down at the blank form on the table in front of her. All around her she could hear the scratches of pencils as the others in the room, following the instructions of the Employment Seminar leader, wrote down their skills, talents, gifts and abilities. Tears filled her eyes, and she desperately wished she'd never come.

Carol reflected on the recent painful move from the home that had been hers for so many years to this unfamiliar city. Memories filled her mind of years spent going the extra mile in her personal fitness and grooming, her homemaking, her meal preparation, and her child-rearing, all trying to infuse life into a marriage that her unfaithful husband had no interest in saving. Where had it brought her? Here—eighteen years later, no husband, five children, no job, and nothing she considered marketable skills. In her grief she laid down her pencil, picked up her purse, and walked out of the seminar.

Grief is the ultimate humbler. It strips us of every thought we ever had that we have any amount of control or power in our lives and lays us low in the dust. Simply living in today's society can be pretty humiliating.

We are surrounded by messages and images of the perfection we may wish we could reach but can't. Then when tragedy takes our spouse, or our marriage fails, and we are in a very obvious way living less than that perfect ideal, we can easily doubt our worth as an individual.

How can we overcome the debilitating effects of grief and feel of worth again? How can we build self-confidence and use our self-talk to build our belief that we *can* move ahead and that our life makes a difference in the world?

In their book, *Parenting Teens with Love and Logic*, authors Foster W. Cline, M.D. and Jim Fay say that teens develop a healthy self-concept through handling responsibility. Could this apply to us with our wounded self-concept as we try to recover from tragic loss? I believe it can, particularly if we realize that it is now our first responsibility to take care of ourselves. The old saying applies: "If momma ain't happy, ain't nobody happy." If *we* aren't doing well, nobody else in the family will be able to heal and move on as well as they could if we were confident and functioning well.

Every time we do something to fulfill that responsibility of self-care, our belief in ourselves will grow, and we will not only be a better example for our children and those around us, but we will feel greater happiness too.

One widow explained it like this: "I slowly realized that I had started to live life in 'victim mode'. People looked at me with sympathy in their eyes. I could feel they were sorry for me, and I began to feel sorry for myself constantly. I felt I couldn't do anything for myself. I let the yard go. I let the house go. Now that I had no one to take care of me—or care for me—I even let myself go. A widow is supposed to look like she's in mourning, right?" She continued, "One day when I looked in the mirror, I realized what I was doing. I didn't want to be the victim anymore. I hated being weak all the time. I wanted to feel strong again. I wanted to believe that I was worth something."

So, what are some specific ways we can build belief in ourselves?

First, think about who you are, and where you came from.

Doreen told me, "It helps me so much to realize that even though I am now alone, I still have a Father in Heaven who cares about me and is watching over me. Somehow I can make it through the hard days if I remind myself that He is near and He loves me."

You are a spiritual being—a child of God. And because that is true, you have divinity within you, and you have a Father who loves you and wants to help you. Ask Him to reveal Himself to you, and to make His hand obvious in your life. Read His words in the scriptures and spend time drawing near to Him in prayer. I have found my greatest strength and my most profound peace when spending time with God.

Second, memorize uplifting words. My favorites are scriptures, but I also continue to add to my collection of poems as the years pass. Then when negative, accusing, demeaning thoughts come to my mind, I can push them out with great quotes. Edgar A. Guest is one of my favorite poets. He somehow captures the ordinary in life and expresses it beautifully. His words give me courage and hope. One of his that I like best follows.

Somebody Said That It Couldn't Be Done

Somebody said that it couldn't be done
But he with a chuckle replied
That "maybe it couldn't," but he would be one
Who wouldn't say so till he tried.
So he buckled right in with the trace of a grin
On his face. If he worried he hid it.
He started to sing as he tackled the thing
That couldn't be done, and he did it!

Somebody scoffed: "Oh, you'll never do that;
At least no one ever has done it";
But he took off his coat and he took off his hat
And the first thing we knew he'd begun it.
With a lift of his chin and a bit of a grin,
Without any doubting or quit-it,
He started to sing as he tackled the thing
That couldn't be done, and he did it.

There are thousands to tell you it cannot be done,
There are thousands to prophesy failure,
There are thousands to point out to you one by one,
The dangers that wait to assail you.
But just buckle in with a bit of a grin,
Just take off your coat and go to it;
Just start in to sing as you tackle the thing
That "cannot be done," and you'll do it.

– EDGAR A. GUEST –

You will find others of my favorites listed in the Appendix. Begin your own list of scriptures, poems, quotes and lyrics that bring you up when you feel down. As you fill your mind and heart with truth, light and uplifting thoughts, you will find your belief in yourself increasing.

Third, if you have children at home, determine to make your home life sweeter.

Amanda's husband was killed instantly in a tragic car accident. She was left with four young children. "I soon saw that my attitude had a huge impact on the children. If I was down and sad, I would be impatient with the children. Then the whole house felt down and sad. So I had to make myself do something, even just one thing, every day, to cheer up the kids. It's made a big difference for all of us."

In your quiet moments of contemplation, decide one or two things you could do each week to make the atmosphere at home more welcoming and less critical. Write notes of appreciation, take time to think of a sincere compliment for each child each day, or find small ways to show you have been thinking of them. Pray for each child and for your relationship with each one. As home life becomes more loving and you feel more successful as a mother, you will become more loving with yourself too.

Fourth, examine how obedient you are to your Heavenly Father. This will require studying His word to know what He is asking of you. What is His standard? How are you doing at living up to it? Disobedience naturally engenders a loss of self-respect and true confidence. As I found ways to increase my obedience, I found my thoughts about myself were more positive. Doing right brings peace and confidence.

Fifth, build others. Your confidence increases as you strive to help another build self-worth. Notice others' strengths and gifts and make a point of telling them when those things bless your life and inspire you. Each time you help someone else feel better about themselves, *you* will feel better about *you*.

Sixth, list your strong points. What are your positive qualities? In *The Five Lessons a Millionaire Taught Me for Women*, Richard Paul Evans says, "one of the traits I often find women guilty of is undervaluing their abilities and talents." Honestly, what was your first thought when you read that first sentence asking you to list your strong points? Did you immediately come up with several to write down? Or did you hear a negative voice saying, "*What* strong points?" Did you have to stop and think?

Ask a friend or trusted relative to tell you the good qualities they have noticed in you and then begin to improve them. Develop a new talent, or research something you've been interested in but have never taken time to study. 1 Corinthians 12 teaches us we each have qualities and gifts that God gave us to help us—and others—through this life. As we seek them and develop them, our sense of worth will grow.

Seventh, where did you come from? What are your roots? Knowing about your ancestors can help you discover who you are and why you have interests in the things you do. I love to garden, and it was sweet to learn that my great-grandmother was well-known for her garden. I love music and playing my violin can fill my soul with peace. It is fun to know that my mother, my grandmother, grandfather, and great-grandfather all played the violin—and passed that love on to me. Another example: I love roses; my Grandma Romney grew and tended a beautiful rose garden each year.

I have always felt something tugging at my heart when I hear bag-pipes. I learned that I have Scottish ancestry, and in my library I have the painting of an ancestor who was an accomplished Scottish dancer, Priscilla Charlotte Clive, posing in her kilt. I like to think that the bag-pipes are calling out to me to remember those who lived before me and to live worthily so that those who come after me can draw strength from my life.

Reading the stories of my ancestors helps "ground" me, and gives me a sense of their hopes for me. They sacrificed much so that their posterity could have the many privileges we have today. As we learn about them, we learn about ourselves at the same time. They are part of us, and knowing them and how they faced their challenges can help us meet the trials we confront.

Eighth, fill your mind with stories of those who have succeeded in spite of difficulty. When I was very young, I would often wake in the night, frightened. I felt small and weak, vulnerable and unable to sleep. I would steal down to the end of the hall where my parents' room was and curl up by their door. They always seemed to have their radio on, and I can remember listening to the voice of the announcer, Earl Nightingale, telling stories of people who had overcome great odds, or stories of people who had done good in the world, and those stories brought peace to my soul. As I lay there dreaming of doing something like that someday, security stole back into my heart, and after awhile I was able to go back to bed and sleep.

Hearing about others who have dealt with difficulty and overcome it can give us courage and help us know we can do it too. I love listening to motivational speakers because they have made it their life's work to find uplifting, motivating stories to help us remember that each human being has worth, and everyone can do something important. I love the confidence I feel after listening to them.

Ninth, dare to dream.

"I'm moving to California!"

Her words took me by surprise, and I stared at her to see if she was really serious. She saw the stunned look on my face. After a terrible divorce, she'd been working part time while pursuing her bachelor's degree, and whenever we were together, most of our conversations had been about the daily challenge of getting by.

She had grown up in California and moved east when she married. She'd always wished she could move back, but was consumed with just making it through each day. Just the day before we had agreed to meet at the symphony to catch up, but I'd never expected to hear this news.

"I know. I never thought I could do it either, but I'm leaving next month," she whispered as the violins in the background finished tuning.

"You'll be living your dream! When did you begin to dream again?" I asked.

"When I realized that the next fifty years of my life are up to me, I decided I want to make them great, and I want to start now."

When you've endured the loss of a loved one, dreams for the future can seem useless. Why go on without that person in your life? What's the use? If your marriage failed, you may see yourself as a failure and be unable to see the possibility for any success in the future.

I believe that we need our dreams now more than ever. We need something to carry us through the darkness and confusion of grief, to help us to build a new life, and give us something to live for. Our dreams can be one thing that helps us to see beyond the present pain and focus on a better day in the future. Dreams motivate us and instill hope. When you nurture a dream, you are creating belief in your ability to change your life for the better.

How do you begin to dream again? Start with a "what if" page in your journal or notebook. Ask yourself some questions and start answering them. *What if I had all the money I could want? What would I do? What if I could go anywhere in the world? Where would I want to go? What if I could take lessons in anything? What would I learn? What if I had the perfect job? What would it look like? What would a perfect day look like?* As you compile the answers to these questions, and any other questions you can think of, you will begin to see dreams materialize. Then you can start to work on them one at a time. As the song from the musical *South Pacific* says, "You gotta have a dream; if you don't have a dream, how you gonna have a dream come true?"

Tenth, create a success filing cabinet. Robert Allen, *New York Times* bestselling author of *The One Minute Millionaire*, suggests one way to build your confidence is to write down every success you've ever had. It could be as far back as a good grade in elementary school or a kind deed you did in your youth. Start listing every good thing about yourself and every success, and create in your mind a filing cabinet that you can open whenever you are discouraged and pull out a positive memory, reliving that moment as vividly as you can. Remember the sights, the sounds, the feelings, the tastes—make it as real as you can. The mind cannot tell the difference between something vividly imagined and something real, so keep remembering past successes and imagining future successes, and your mind will begin to propel you toward further achievements, believing you are a person of success.

As we work on these things, we will come to the point where we believe that, in and of ourselves, we have value and that we are important. We are here, still alive, and that fact alone can give us hope that there is something we can do to make the world better. As we contribute our small part, it will bring us a sense of accomplishment, and accelerate our healing. Believe it.

Essential Tasks for Building Belief in Yourself

- Remind yourself daily that you are a child of God. He doesn't make mistakes; you were given everything you need to succeed, with His help. Draw near to Him, and ask Him in prayer to help you understand your worth. You *are* valuable!

- Make a list of every single success in your life from as far back as you can remember. Keep adding to it as more successes come to mind. Read this list frequently.

- Compile a list of your good qualities and review it often. See how these qualities equip you to make a difference in the world around you, even in small ways. Solicit the input of others to help you see the ways you impact others positively.

- Begin to dream. Make a page in your journal just to write down dreams you'd love to see realized. Re-read this page often, and allow yourself to vividly imagine those dreams coming true.

- Use affirmations daily. Determine automatic reminders to repeat them—every time the phone rings, the doorbell rings, at the top of every hour, etc. Post them around your home. Make your own list of affirmations or choose some from the Appendix or my Web site www.roslynreynolds.com.

CHAPTER ELEVEN

SERVE

If I can stop one heart from breaking,
I shall not live in vain;
If I can ease one life the aching,
Or cool one pain,
Or help one fainting robin
Unto his nest again,
I shall not live in vain.

— EMILY DICKINSON —

"Please come back again. Come soon!"

Her soft, wrinkled hands gripped my hand, her pale blue eyes fixed on mine. "We need more groups like yours. Please come back!"

Her pleading touched my heart. Could our half-hour program really have been that meaningful to her?

I turned from the last resident to leave the room and closed the clasps on my violin case. I cringed to think of the missed notes, the hesitant beginning to the piece we had decided to add at the last minute, and my stumbling introductions to the group. The microphone hadn't functioned properly, so my voice had been either inaudible or had thundered through the room making the residents jump in their chairs.

I hadn't had time to coordinate completely with the other family so we had exchanged a few hurried thoughts about the program as we were setting up, and then it just kind of fell into place as we sang and played each number. Several last-minute changes and additions made it a completely different program than I had had in mind, although the children each performed well. It hadn't been *my* best performance.

Yet they wanted us back.

The children were now smiling, laughing amongst one another as we trooped from the care center. Many had entered grumbling, complaining that I'd arranged again for them to come. Yet it always ended this way—happy, light-hearted, touched by the gratitude of so many dear people for our simple offering.

This was what made life sweet. Knowing that I had made a difference in someone's life that day erased all the worries I had entered with, if even for an hour, and the tender feeling that lingered in my heart would be there forever.

We had presented a similar program at a community hospital just six months after Marty had died, and afterward while we were greeting the patients, a man approached me with tears in his eyes and with difficulty asked halting between each word, "How . . . did . . . you . . . do . . . that?"

I was confused by his question, and a woman standing next to him explained that he had recently lost his wife, and he wanted to know how I could be out in public, composed and presenting programs while still grieving the loss of my spouse.

I could only answer that we *had* to be there. We had to find ways to get outside our pain or we would be consumed with our own grief. Coming to the hospital hopefully brightened the patients' lives, but it assuredly brightened ours. We cannot come away from those places without having been lifted and without counting our blessings. We are reminded that truly every person has value. We are reminded that those who are confined need interaction and love. And our memories are awakened to the many blessings we do have, that others have struggles far worse than ours—and that we have the ability to lighten their burdens. The more often we remember those things, the happier our lives can be.

In speaking with other women who have endured loss, I have been inspired by the diverse ways they have found to reach out to serve. Cathy went through the shock of betrayal, a painful divorce, and now has the entire burden of providing a living for herself and her daughter. She has gone back to school to pursue a degree in psychology, and her time is filled to capacity with necessities. However, she has chosen to volunteer with Safe Harbor, a domestic violence women's shelter where women and children can come for help.

Knowing she must see a lot of pain and tragedy, I asked her if it wasn't hard to deal with her own grief, and then to spend her spare time being surrounded by so much misery. Her answer touched me deeply.

"Yes, it is hard. But I can remember seeing my mother beaten, and being so young and powerless, I couldn't do a thing to help her. If I can now do for other women what I couldn't do for my mother, I want to do it."

She continued, "If I have learned one thing from my painful experience, it is that I cannot change anyone else. However, I can help others by giving them comfort, understanding, and direction, and if I can help just one person, it will be worth it."

The philosopher Albert Schweitzer said, "You must give some time to your fellow man. Even if it's a little thing, do something for those who have need of help, something for which you get no pay but the privilege of doing it."

"The only ones among you who will be really happy are those who will have sought and found how to serve."

One day I received a phone call from my friend Sue.

"Ros, my family and I would like to do something for you. I have a brother who works in construction and remodels homes, and we'd like to do a makeover on your bedroom and bathroom. Would you be willing to let us do that?"

Willing? It was what I had wanted to do since we had moved into this home, but I'd had no idea how I could ever accomplish it. Now here was someone offering to do it for me. I accepted her offer, thrilled, and the next week her whole family came to join in the project. I answered the door and there stood Sue, her father, her sister and brother-in-law, and their son.

I'd rarely seen a happier group of people. Their faces glowed, and they radiated excitement and eagerness to be about their work. I felt a longing to be like that—to be thinking about others, and to be out in the world making a difference. A hope entered my heart—*Maybe someday, maybe when this is all over and I feel human again, I can be like them.*

I invited them in and after introductions they all walked down the hall to my room, took out their supplies, and started right into work.

Down came the old mirrored squares that had been glued on the wall, the thick wallpaper, the cracked light switch covers and the old light fixtures. Several days in a row they returned, scraping the walls, repairing the damage of forty years of living and making them smooth and ready to paint. Then they brought in a paint sprayer, and in three days the walls looked like those of a brand-new model home.

The next day Sue and her father arrived with electrical tools and beautiful new light fixtures for my room and the master bathroom. They worked most of the day installing the fixtures and getting the outlets in order. At one point Sue had to leave to get something, and I went in and visited with her father as he worked.

"Tell me about your family," he asked. I told him of our beginnings, and about each child. I asked about his family, and he told me about some of the trials he had experienced in his life. He had lost his wife years earlier, and he spoke of how she had always loved to help other people, and how he now found comfort in finding ways to serve. In the course of the conversation he said something that I have remembered ever since.

"I've discovered that life is all about problems and learning to overcome them and live on in spite of them. Anyone who thinks that we are here to figure out how to live without problems has a lot to learn!"

Years ago I would have thought that to be a pessimistic attitude. Now, because of these friends and my own experience, I see the wisdom in approaching life from that viewpoint. If we know that we are here to experience difficulty and to grow through learning how to face and overcome it, then every problem becomes a stepping stone instead of a roadblock.

We settled into silence for a few moments, and I was deeply touched to watch him working away, knowing there would be no reward or payment for what he was doing other than my enduring gratitude. I felt so grateful to have been blessed with such friends around me. Could there be a truer meaning of friendship than to sacrifice for another's good?

The following week, Sue provided the final touch. She and her sister purchased a beautiful new bedspread and pillows for my bed, a wall shelf with flowers and a figurine, a painting of the Savior, and she framed two watercolors my daughter had painted.

When the project was finished and I walked into that room, it was as if I was stepping into a new phase of life. All the reminders of past pain and difficulty were erased, and everything in that room reminded me of newness, hope, and the sweetness—and power—of friendship.

In her book, *How to Make a Difference*, Catherine E. Poelman counsels, " . . . start small, simply remember that everyone in this world has the same basic need: to love and to be loved. Each individual is a child of God; human kinship is our connection to each other; and serving another person is an act of love."

Mrs. Poelman's message is manna for the woman who is grieving and is tied down to a job and taking care of the home, the children, and all that those roles entail, and wonders, *Is there time for service? Do I have even an ounce of energy left to give to something outside my own obligations and commitments?*

Even very small acts make a difference. Some of the smallest things I have done have brought the sweetest moments into my life. I remember walking past an elderly neighbor's home and feeling I should stop and visit. I really didn't have time; my children were waiting for me at home; but the feeling was strong, so I turned my steps toward her front door.

She answered with a delighted smile and took me into her kitchen to show me the photos of her grandchildren she had just received in the mail. She glowed as she shared her pride in their accomplishments, and her words tumbled out as she expressed gratitude for her descendants.

She needed to share with someone; I needed to forget my own problems for a few minutes, and when we parted moments later, we both felt blessed. Sweet moments like that give us solace as we work through our healing.

Another time, the name of a widow in my neighborhood kept coming to mind. I knew I needed to write her a note. Although I was pressed for time, I went to the closet, chose a note card, and sat down at the dining room table and wrote. The words seemed to flow onto the paper, telling her she was valued and loved, thanking her for her influence in my life. It took only a couple of minutes, but when I was done, I felt a wave of approval and peace. Those had not been my words; God wanted to send this daughter of His a message and had used my hands to write it down and send it to her. I had been a partner with God in doing something that would make a difference in someone's life, and it felt good.

The temptation is always great to think I do not have time to listen to those whisperings that invite me into that partnership with God, but every time I have hearkened and taken time out to follow them, I have been lifted and blessed. God is not only filling someone else's need when I do His bidding, He is filling my needs too.

President Spencer W. Kimball said in an address to the Rotary Club, "Only when you lift a burden, God will lift your burden. Divine paradox this! The man who staggers and falls because his burden is too great can lighten that burden by taking on the weight of another's burden. You get by giving, but your part of giving must be given first."

President Kimball was a man who practiced what he preached. I observed him one evening at a garden wedding reception. Marty and I were out in the front yard of my Aunt's home where the reception was being held when we saw him getting out of a car that had just pulled up to the curb. A security man followed and stayed nearby, watching intently those around him the entire time. As we watched, President Kimball walked up the driveway, went through the line and greeted the wedding party, and then before leaving, took a plate of refreshments and turning, gave it to the security man who had accompanied him. His thoughts were ever on serving others.

So start small. Make a phone call. Keep an eye out for someone who might need a note. Just the fact that our eyes are looking outward for a few moments can lift us out of our own despair for that short time and we are blessed. I believe God blesses us for trying to reach out and get beyond our problems. I have experienced a lighter heart, and I have felt inklings that there is something greater than just surviving that I need to do. Each time I reach out in small ways, I feel blessed to be God's hands or eyes or ears for that short time, and it brings a sweetness to life that is not there otherwise.

I know how it feels to be deep in grief. Some days I found it hard to think of one thing I had to give to the world. When you have those days it helps to have a list of your talents, no matter how small or insignificant they may seem to you, because as you look over that list with a prayer in your heart, you may come up with a new idea of a way you can serve someone else.

My list is pretty basic. I can read, so I could read a book or story to someone. I am comfortable singing as long as I'm in a group. I can weed a garden. I enjoy reciting poetry. I'm good at cleaning house. I listen well. I can smile. I am tolerable at the piano and violin. I can write a letter. And yes, I do windows.

None of those things are terribly impressive, but each of them could fill a simple need. As you begin your list, focus on the basics. Somehow it doesn't seem so overwhelming to decide to reach out to others if you can do something simple. Then, as you do one thing and experience the joy that comes because of it, you may feel more capable of doing even more.

I made a study of after-life experiences a few years ago. The stories intrigued me, and I was touched by the fact that a great majority of them had a similar resolution: the person who "died" and then was allowed to come back and live more of life was told to go back and serve. They all came back with a mission, something they knew they must accomplish before their time on earth was complete. That mission was never "Go build an empire," "Become famous and powerful," but rather the common thread was "Go be a better father or mother, a better spouse and neighbor. Be Christ-like, and tell others that every moment of life matters. Use each day to make a difference."

The Holy Bible teaches in Deuteronomy 10:12: " . . . serve the Lord thy God with all thy heart and with all thy soul." How do we keep that commandment? How can we serve One we cannot see, and One who is omnipotent? What does He need our service for?

The Savior gives us part of the answer in John 12:26: "If any man serve me, let him follow me."

How do we follow Him? What did He spend his time doing? In Acts 10:38, Paul tells us Christ "went about doing good."

There lies our answer. If we are to serve God, we must follow the example of our Savior and do good. Paul exhorted the Galatians, "By love serve one another."

When I review all that was done for me during the days surrounding the funeral, I find countless acts of service. Truly people were following Christ, doing good, and serving my family. As they did, we felt His love filling our hearts and lifting us, carrying us through our darkest hours.

The quickest way to overcome the tendency to dwell on our own problems is to spend some time helping others to forget theirs. There is healing in finding a new reason to live, a way to give to the world and to know that the world is better for you having been there. Go ahead. Brighten someone's day and feel better yourself too.

ESSENTIALS FOR SERVING

- Start making your list of talents, abilities, and gifts you have that you can use to serve and help others. Remember the simpler the better.

- See the Appendix for a list of Web sites, service organizations, humanitarian causes and books that can spark ideas for ways to reach out and help someone else.

- Determine a time each month to dedicate to service, and then pray for ideas and opportunities to fill that time.

- Determine to accept inconvenient chances to serve.

- Begin each day with a prayer to open your eyes to opportunities to serve. Listen for the promptings of the Spirit directing you to those who might need you.

EPILOGUE

Solo? In truth, my title is inaccurate. I have come to know that we are never truly alone as we walk this new path that is ours each day. If we feel alone, it is because we have drawn ourselves away from Him who promised, "I will not leave you comfortless; I will come to you." He *is* there. Of that I am a witness.

Getting It All Together? Again I must admit that is misleading. I cannot say I have it all together, even yet. However, I have found peace. I have learned that our souls must heal even as our bodies after injury, and that submitting to and working through the pain required to allow that healing can be cleansing, rejuvenating, and sanctifying.

Yes, tragic things have happened to us. But we are not alone. There are others near us who have suffered too, and who will help to bear us up. And there is joy, warmth, peace and fulfillment ahead if we will put ourselves in God's hands, follow where He leads, and allow His healing hand to make of us what He will.

What is my last advice to someone experiencing loss? Draw near to God. Seek Him. Be willing to lay everything on the altar and submit to His greater plan in your life. As you do that, He can work miracles in your life. I know. He is doing so in mine.

APPENDIX

When Tragedy Strikes: A To-Do List

When we experience the death of a loved one, we most often react in shock. Because it can be difficult to think clearly, I offer here a list of tasks and ideas that may help you to move through the first hours and days following your loss. May they prove to be helpful, and may you feel God's nearness as you navigate this stormy sea of grief. I'll begin with a checklist you can use over the next few days, and then explain each one in more detail.

___Pray—often!

___Take care of yourself

___Be aware of the children's needs

___Gather support

___Make burial arrangements

___Make phone calls—family, friends, etc.

___Plan funeral and viewings

___Gather information for obituary

___List tasks you could use help with

___Get basic finances in order

___Plan time together

1. **Pray!** God knows your need, and He can give you strength and courage you can find in no other way. Trust that He knows how to succor you, and ask for His guidance through this difficult time.

2. **Take care of yourself.** Sit down. Take a deep breath. Take a drink of water. Realize you need to take care of yourself to get through this. You may not feel like eating or drinking, but to keep from becoming even more drained and exhausted, you must force yourself to take in enough nutrition to keep your energy up. When things get overwhelming, allow yourself to rest.

3. **Children.** Take time, even if it is just a few moments, to be alone with the children and re-connect each day. There is so much to do to prepare for a funeral, and we are still so in shock that it is easy to forget to take time for the children. Make them a priority. They need you while they are grieving. Are there any of your children who need special attention? Is there a friend or relative who could be near for them while you are involved with the necessary preparations?

4. **Gather support.** Who do you know that can help you? Do you have a sibling, a parent, a close friend? Someone who can make calls for you and answer the door, bring you plates of food, notice when you are exhausted and take over for you so you can rest?

5. **Set up a time to make burial arrangements.** This will most likely be done with the mortuary that cares for the body of your loved one. Plot, casket, vault and grave liner all need to be chosen. A wise funeral director can give good advice about what is really necessary and what expenses are excessive.

6. **Make necessary calls letting people know what has happened.** People you will want to notify immediately:
   - Family members
   - Close friends
   - Church leaders
   - His employer and work associates

Once the funeral arrangements have been made, calls can be made to those in your address book—all who knew your loved one and would want to attend the services. If you desire, have someone do this for you. My mind was so occupied with visitors and making arrangements, and my emotions were so unpredictable that I gladly accepted my oldest daughter's offer to make these calls for me.

Other calls that may need to be made:
- Teachers and administrators at the children's schools
- Coaches, music teachers, etc.
- Appointments you had that need to be cancelled or postponed

7. **Planning the Funeral Program.** Usually the funeral director oversees all of this. It is helpful to have access to the names of your extended family to draw from as you plan. Choose a location, speakers, prayers, organists, musical numbers and accompanists. Choose pall bearers and honorary pall bearers. Let the children be as involved as they want to be. Allowing them to participate helps them to more fully comprehend what has happened, and to find closure. I offered all of my children the chance to participate in the funeral; of the seven children, four chose to be on the program, and three chose to stay seated in the audience with me. However, all participated in choosing what would be included in the program.

8. **Information to gather.** Obituary information—the newspaper has an outline to fill in. You may want to include any professional titles and roles your spouse held, list any special accomplishments you want to mention, and anything that captures his personality and the impact he had on you and all those his life touched. You will need to include the date and time of the funeral services.

9. **Make lists of specific things you need help with.** Share these needs with those who offer to help and with the leader of your religious congregation. People really will feel better if you let them help.

    Before the funeral and for the days surrounding the services
    - Accommodations for out-of-town guests
    - Clothing and shoes for you and the children for the funeral— does anything need to be laundered, repaired, taken to the cleaners or purchased?

- Meals for your family
- Laundry
- Home straightening/organizing
- Yard care, snow removal, etc.
- Arrange for someone to sit in your home during the funeral

After the funeral and long-term projects

When tragedy strikes, people want to help, but many have no idea what they can do for you. It helps to ease their grief if they can do something they feel would be useful to you. Begin a list of things in the home that need to be fixed—leaky faucets, broken appliances, drawers and hinges that need repair, etc. Include organizational projects, too. Then when someone says, "What can I do to help?" you can turn to these lists, and they can choose what they have the skills and talents to do. This helps them to feel useful, and it is helpful to you because the projects you need help with will be addressed. Take advantage of everyone's generosity at this time. Allowing them to perform a service for you will bless their life as well as yours.

10. **Financial.** Has your mortgage payment been paid this month? Have the utilities? How about all the basic monthly bills? Have someone help you get these things taken care of. You will not be thinking clearly for a while, and it is easy to forget to get these paid on time. Consider withdrawing some money to get you by until things get settled, in case a bank puts a hold on your account.

11. **Time together.** Lastly, consider taking time after the funeral to be together with your family away from the phone and doorbell for a day or two just to grow closer together and to make some good memories before you go back to the day-to-day requirements of life. My brother and sister-in-law provided a hotel room in a nearby city,

and we took a 'mini-vacation.' We went swimming, went out to dinner, went roller-skating, and played games in the hotel room. It was a time we all enjoyed, and a memory we cherish, when we were able to have some fun together, smile once more, and to grow in our love for each other.

SUMMARY

Tackling these lists and tasks may seem overwhelming, but as you get all of this down on paper, you will begin to see that with small steps, everything can be accomplished that needs to be. Without writing it down, it can seem like a huge weight, impossible to bear. Determine a place to keep these lists, perhaps in a small notebook, and keep adding to them. Check off items completed, and as you begin to see progress, you will realize you can accomplish things even when your grief is overwhelming and you feel you can't do anything.

Remember Philippians 4:13: "I can do all things through Christ which strengtheneth me." This will be hard—maybe the hardest thing you've ever done—but with God, and with friends around you, you can do it.

Resources and Organizations dealing with Grief

- The leader of your local church congregation is a good place to start. Some of the very best counsel and greatest comfort I've received have come from my bishop.

- Check your local newspaper in the community calendar area for a nearby grief group. Most communities have a group that meets weekly.

- In addition, check out some of the following online resources:

www.griefsteps.com

www.griefhealing.com

www.opentohope.com
Open to Hope Foundation
188 Minna Street
San Francisco, CA 94105

www.griefnet.org
GriefNet
PO Box 3272
Ann Arbor, MI 48106-3272

http://grief.net/
Grief Recovery Institute
PO Box 6061-382
Sherman Oaks, CA 91413

www.griefshare.org
GriefShare
PO Box 1739
Wake Forest, NC 27588

Books I Found Especially Helpful

I Wasn't Ready To Say Goodbye by Brooke Noel & Pamela D. Blair, PhD

Grieving, The Pain and the Promise by Deanna Edwards

Widow to Widow by Genevieve Davis Ginsburg, M.S.

A Grief Observed by C.S. Lewis

Widowed by Dr. Joyce Brothers

If Thou Endure it Well by Neal A. Maxwell

The Gateway We Call Death by Russell M. Nelson

Living When a Loved One Has Died by Rabbi Earl Grollman

Suggested Musical Selections

Though it would take a whole book to list all the music I love, this is a small sample of the pieces and collections of classical and other music that I can listen to and immediately have my spirits lifted and calmed. Choose your favorites and begin compiling your own list of great musical 'perks.'

CLASSICAL
- Rachmaninoff—Sonata for Cello and Piano in G Minor, Movement 3 "Andante"
- Rachmaninoff—any of his piano concertos
- Sibelius—*Finlandia*
- Piano concertos by Grieg, Liszt, Tchaikovsky, Mendelssohn and Chopin
- Violin Concertos by Bruch, Brahms, Bloch, Barber, Mendelssohn, Beethoven, Bach
- Holst—The Planets
- Dvorak—New World Symphony
- Brahms—Any of his waltzes
- Handel—Water Music

INSPIRATIONAL
- CDs by the Mormon Tabernacle Choir, especially *Then Sings My Soul, Peace Like a River, Consider the Lilies, Love Is Spoken Here*
- *Bryn Terfel Sings Favorites*
- Handel—*The Messiah*

FUN
- Prokofieff—*Peter and the Wolf*
- Saint-Saens—*Carnival of the Animals*
- Mormon Tabernacle Choir—*Showtime*
- John Williams—*Olympic Fanfare and Theme for the Olympic Games*
- Aaron Copland—*Fanfare for the Common Man, Appalachian Spring, Rodeo*
- Musical Soundtracks—*Sound of Music, Brigadoon, My Fair Lady, etc.*

Suggested Books

This is a smattering of some of my favorite books (besides the scriptures) to reach for when I need a lift. Though many are considered children's books, I feel they have value for the tender stories, excellent writing, and inspiring messages they share. Many of these are books my children and I read in the evenings, and they are sure to leave you feeling uplifted when you finish. If you can't get out of the 'slumps', reach for a good book. See my Web site, www.roslynreynolds.com for more.

Cheaper by the Dozen by Frank Gilbreth, Jr.

Laddie by Gene Stratton Porter

Chronicles of Narnia by CS Lewis

Jane Eyre by Charlotte Bronte

Screwtape Letters by CS Lewis

101 Dalmations by Dodie Smith

Little Britches Series by Ralph Moody

Anne of Green Gables Series by Lucy Maude Montgomery

God's Smuggler by Brother Andrew

Tramp for the Lord by Corrie Ten Boom

Ten Peas in a Pod by Arnold Pent III

Where the Red Fern Grows by Wilson Rawls

Pollyanna by Eleanor H. Porter

Magnificent Obsession by Lloyd C. Douglas

Charlotte's Web by EB White

Yearning for the Living God by F. Enzio Busche

The Princess and Curdie by George MacDonald

The Princess and the Goblin by George MacDonald

The Story of My Life by Helen Keller

Little Women by Louisa May Alcott

Big Red by Jim Kjelgaard

Incredible Journey by Sheila Burnford

In His Steps by Charles M. Sheldon

Pride and Prejudice by Jane Austen

Rebecca of Sunnybrook Farm by Kate Douglas

Johnny Tremain by Esther Forbes

Hans Brinker by Mary Mapes Dodge

Bronze Bow by Elizabeth George Speare

Father Flanagan of Boys' Town by Fulton Oursler and Will Oursler

James Herriott books

Mama's Bank Account by Katherine Forbes

A Christmas Carol by Charles Dickens

Great Expectations by Charles Dickens

David Copperfield by Charles Dickens

Joy Breaks by Clairmont, Johnson, Meberg and Swindoll

Gift from the Sea by Anne Morrow Lindbergh

Ruth's Hospital Room Quotes

These are taken from the posters Ruth Romney Powell hangs in her hospital room each time she goes in for surgery, and they serve not only to brighten her day but also that of each person who enters her room. See my Web site, www.roslynreynolds.com for more.

Give me patience—I need it RIGHT NOW!

Smile! If you can't raise the outer edges of your mouth, at least droop your lower lip!

Laugh and the world laughs with you—cry and you get wet!

Remember even Moses was once a basket case!

When we choose a path we also choose its built-in destination.

Of all the things I've lost, I miss my mind the most.

My mind works like lightning—one brilliant flash and it's gone!

If you can't be grateful for what you receive, be grateful for what you escape! *—EB Romney 1918-1998*

Where there's a will, there's always a relative.

If you could spank the person responsible for most of your problems, you would not be able to sit down for a month! *—J. Golden Kimball 1863-1937*

A merry heart doeth good like a medicine. *Proverbs 17:22*

I finally got it all together but I forgot where I put it.

Do not bemoan getting older . . . many are denied the opportunity.

Too bad life isn't like a VCR so you could fast-forward through the yucky parts!

Affirmations

These are simply phrases I repeat to myself when negative thoughts come crowding onto the stage of my mind. Use them to inspire your own 'pick-me-ups' that will bolster your courage and build your faith when darkness threatens to conquer your spirits.

"For God hath not given us the spirit of fear, but of power, and of love, and of a sound mind." *2 Timothy 1:7*

"Fear thou not; for I am with thee: be not dismayed; for I am thy God: I will strengthen thee; yea I will help thee; yea I will uphold thee with the right hand of my righteousness." *Isaiah 41:10*

"Rest in the Lord, and wait patiently for him; fret not . . ." *Psalms 37:7*

"I can do all things through Christ which strengtheneth me." *Phiippians 4:13*

"When we put God first, all other things fall into their proper place or drop out of our lives. Our love of the Lord will govern the claims for our affection, the demands on our time, the interests we pursue, and the order of our priorities." *—Ezra Taft Benson, 1988*

"Be still and know that I am God." *Psalms 46:10*

". . . when ye are in the service of your fellow beings ye are only in the service of your God." *Mosiah 2:17*

"This is my commandment, That ye love one another, as I have loved you." *John 15:12*

". . . the fruit of the Spirit is love, joy, peace, longsuffering, gentleness, goodness, faith, meekness, temperance . . ." *Galatians 5:22-23*

"Let the peace of God rule in your hearts . . . let the word of Christ dwell in you richly . . ." *Colossians 3:12-17*

". . . all things work together for good to them that love God . . ." *Romans 8:28*

With God at my side, all things are possible.

I am God's child. There is divinity within me! I will live to honor that divinity.

Resources for Service Opportunities

- *How To Make a Difference*, Poelman, Catherine; Shadow Mountain, 2002 (This book has a wealth of information on service opportunities in a great variety of fields. I challenge anyone to read this book and not find at least one way they would be excited to serve!)

- www.volunteermatch.org

- www.usa.gov/Citizen/Topics/PublicService.shtml

- www.ed.gov/students/involve/service/edpicks.jhtml

- www.specialolympics.org

- www.nationalabilitycenter.org

- www.literacyvolunteers.org

- Google "Volunteer Opportunities" and then enter your city name. Depending on the size of your city, you may need to enter the name of a larger nearby city.

- Check with your local church congregation leaders. They often will know of service opportunities in your neighborhood.

- Call your town or city offices. There are usually many volunteer opportunities available in your local area.

- Call your local community center, hospital, assisted living center, or rest home. They have frequent need for volunteers on a one-time basis, and on-going opportunities also.

Poems

This list gives you an idea of the type of poem I love to collect and keep fresh in my mind to keep my thoughts positive and directed toward others rather than focused on my challenges. See my Web site, www.roslyn-reynolds.com for more.

Sonnet, William Wordsworth

Christmas Everywhere, Phillips Brooks

The Builders, Henry Wadsworth Longfellow

The Psalm of Life, Henry Wadsworth Longfellow

Be Strong, Maltbie Davenport Babcock

How Did You Die? Edmund Vance Cooke

Mercy, Shakespeare (from "Merchant of Venice")

If, Rudyard Kipling

Keep A-Goin', Frank L. Stanton

The Spider and the Fly, Mary Howitt

Home, Edgar A. Guest

The Road Not Taken, Robert Frost

A Time to Talk, Robert Frost

Others, Charles D. Meigs

God Answers Prayers, Eliza M. Hickok

Be the Best of Whatever You Are, Douglas Malloch

Fix Your Finances Forms

Financial Accounts/Assets

BANK ACCOUNT 1

_____

Financial Institution Name

_____

Account Number/Name   Type of Account

_____

Phone Number   Date opened/purchased

_____

Balance / Rate of Return   Date of Maturity

_____

Co-signers

BANK ACCOUNT 2

_____

Financial Institution Name

_____

Account Number/Name   Type of Account

_____

Phone Number   Date opened/purchased

_____

Balance / Rate of Return   Date of Maturity

_____

Co-signers

Financial Accounts/Assets

BANK ACCOUNT 3

_____

Financial Institution Name

_____

Account Number/Name   Type of Account

_____

Phone Number   Date opened/purchased

_____

Balance / Rate of Return   Date of Maturity

_____

Co-signers

BANK ACCOUNT 4

_____

Financial Institution Name

_____

Account Number/Name   Type of Account

_____

Phone Number   Date opened/purchased

_____

Balance / Rate of Return   Date of Maturity

_____

Co-signers

Insurance

LIFE INSURANCE

Company Name   Type of Policy

Agent Name / Phone Number   Amount of Policy

Policy Number   Monthly Payment

Beneficiaries / those covered by policy

HEALTH INSURANCE

Company Name

Agent Name / Phone Number

Policy Number   Monthly Payment

Beneficiaries / those covered by policy

Insurance

DENTAL INSURANCE

_____

Company Name

_____

Agent Name / Phone Number

_____

Policy Number   Monthly Payment

_____

Beneficiaries / those covered by policy

EYE INSURANCE

_____

Company Name

_____

Agent Name / Phone Number

_____

Policy Number   Monthly Payment

_____

Beneficiaries / those covered by policy

Insurance

AUTO INSURANCE

_____

Company Name

_____

Agent Name / Phone Number

_____

Policy Number   Monthly Payment

_____

Vehicles covered by policy

HOME INSURANCE

_____

Company Name

_____

Agent Name / Phone Number

_____

Policy Number   Monthly Payment

Debts / Liabilities

	Bank / Debtor Name	Balance Owed	Monthly Payment	# Months Remaining	Due Date
Mortgage					
Auto 1					
Auto 2					
Auto 3					
Credit Card 1					
Credit Card 2					
Credit Card 3					
Credit Card 4					
Medical Bills					
Medical Bills					
Other					
Other					

Names of Financial Professionals

CPA

_____

Company Name

_____

Name   Phone Number

_____

Email Address

PERSONAL BANKER

_____

Company Name

_____

Name   Phone Number

_____

Email Address

ATTORNEY

_____
Company Name

_____
Name   Phone Number

_____
Email Address

FINANCIAL ADVISOR

_____
Company Name

_____
Name   Phone Number

_____
Email Address

STOCKBROKER

_____
Company Name

_____
Name   Phone Number

_____
Email Address

Physicians, Caregivers

OPHTHALMOLOGIST

_____

Name

_____

Phone Number   Email Address

_____

Street Address

OPTICIAN

_____

Name

_____

Phone Number   Email Address

_____

Street Address

DENTIST

_____
Name

_____
Phone Number   Email Address

_____
Street Address

M.D.

_____
Name

_____
Phone Number   Email Address

_____
Street Address

SPECIALIST

_____
Name

_____
Phone Number   Email Address

_____
Street Address

Documents to Gather

Location	Document
	Passports
	Birth Certificates
	Copies of Drivers' Licenses
	Estate Plan/Trust/Will *(See next page)*
	Social Security Cards
	Death Certificates
	Marriage Certificate
	Property Deed; Mortgage Papers
	Auto Titles
	Post Office Box information and keys
	Safe Deposit Box *(See Below)
	Subscription records
	Residential Inventory
	Armed Service Discharge Papers
	Funeral Plans
	Computer Passwords

APPENDIX: IMPORTANT FORMS AND INFORMATION

Estate Plan/Trust/Will

Type   Date Executed

Name of Testator

Location of Original   Location of Copy

Personal Representative   Phone Number

Trustee   Trustee

Trustee   Trustee

Guardian   Gaurdian

Guardian   Gaurdian

Power of Attorney

Date of Last Codicil

Prepared by

Safety Deposit Box

_____

Bank Name

_____

Address

_____

Phone Number

_____

Box Number   Date Opened

_____

Authorized signers

_____

Persons with Keys

Inventory

_____   _____

Item   Date Deposited

_____   _____

Item   Date Deposited

_____   _____

Item   Date Deposited

_____   _____

Item   Date Deposited

_____   _____

Item   Date Deposited

Investments

MONEY MARKET

Institution Name

Account Number / Name — Date opened

Balance / Rate of Return — Date of Maturity

Co-signers

Co-signers

IRA

Institution Name

Account Number / Name — Date opened

Balance / Rate of Return — Date of Maturity

Co-signers

Co-signers

RETIREMENT ACCOUNT

Institution Name   Type of Investment

Account Number / Name   Date opened

Balance / Rate of Return   Date of Maturity

Co-signers

Beneficiaries

OTHER INVESTMENTS

Institution Name

Account Number / Name   Date opened   Initial Investment

Balance / Rate of Return   Date of Maturity

Co-signers

Beneficiaries

STOCKS 1

Broker Name

Stock Name

Location of Certificate   Initial Investment

Number of Shares   Price per Share

Commission   Total Investment

STOCKS 2

Broker Name

Stock Name

Location of Certificate   Initial Investment

Number of Shares   Price per Share

Commission   Total Investment

Occupation Information

_____

Employer Name

_____

Phone Number

_____

Email

_____

Address

_____

Employer Name

_____

Phone Number

_____

Email

_____

Address

Business Owned

Financial Accounts held at

Account Numbers

Shareholders, co-owners, etc. (Name/Phone/Email)

Shareholders, co-owners, etc. (Name/Phone/Email)

Shareholders, co-owners, etc. (Name/Phone/Email)

Shareholders, co-owners, etc. (Name/Phone/Email)

Product Storage Location

Other Business Contacts

Other Business Contacts

Other Business Contacts

Other Business Contacts

Monthly Bills

ITEM	Due Date	Owed To Company / Name	Amount	Balance if applicable
Tithing				
Savings				
Mortgage				
Home Insurance				
Auto Payment				
Auto Insurance				
Utilities / Gas				
Water				
Phone				
Cell Phone				
Internet				
Cable/Satellite				
Health Insurance				
Credit Card				
Credit Card				
Other				
Other				

ACKNOWLEDGMENTS

To a loving Heavenly Father from whom I gain my greatest strength; To Mom and Dad, for the gift of life, and for instilling a love of words and books;

To my siblings Ruth and Theo, Fred and Pat, Clive and Bonnie, Stan, Eldon and Lynda, RaeLynne and Brian and Vince and Chriss, for constant love, support and encouragement—and needed correction;

To Marty for every great moment of our twenty-eight years;

To Richard Paul Evans and Robert G. Allen whose challenge in October 2007 inspired me to start writing;

To Karen Christoffersen for her outstanding editing, and for her sweet companionship on the all-too-often lonely path of widowhood;

To Fran Platt for a design beyond my greatest hopes;

To Joycebelle Edelbrock and Dian Thomas for sterling examples and untiring mentoring;

To Michael Wolsey and Jennilyn McKinnon whose weekly prodding on our Mastermind calls kept me on track;

To Lengel, Kim and all my Bountiful sisterhood for continually asking, "How's the book coming?" keeping me at work so I could report any little progress;

To RaeLynne and Brian for opening their home to the children all the times I had to be away;

To Rabbi Earl Grollman for his belief in my project;

To Rick for telling me I did have something worthwhile to say;

To Bob for encouraging me out of my cocoon; ("Fly, Butterfly!")

To my fellow WriteWise authors for their constant encouragement and kudos for each small accomplishment on the way to seeing this completed;

And especially to the brave women who share this journey and who shared their stories with me—I give thanks and appreciation. Without any one of you, this book would not have been possible.

About the Author

ROSLYN ROMNEY REYNOLDS, born sixth in a family of nine children, was raised in a musical family. Some of her favorite memories are of performing in ensembles with her siblings and parents, from string duets to family vocal performances. Her least favorite—and most terrifying performances—were solo.

When she married, she thoroughly enjoyed the companionship that marriage brought. Now, she'd never be 'solo' again! She recalls one day as a newlywed, seeing an elderly couple walking hand in hand, and thinking, "That's going to be us in fifty years."

That dream was cut short. Her husband drowned on a family outing and she felt totally unprepared for the 'solo' life. With numerous elderly relatives, attending funerals had been an accepted part of her growing-up years. She came to view them as comforting family gatherings, filled with love. But her husband's death was different, and she felt confused and frightened. Their seven children became her greatest incentive to learn how to move through the grieving process and on to find new purpose in life.

Now she is building a new life for herself and her family. She has started a home-based business, become an author, and has made many new friends in the process. She finds great joy in being with her children and grandchildren, traveling, camping, reading, playing games, and finding new places to visit and new ways to serve.

Her dream is to make a difference in the world by lifting hearts and giving hope to those who may feel hopeless, encouraging them to discover that the greatest way to heal is to find a cause greater than oneself.